The Prisoner of

or, Captain Hayward's "I

Harry Hazelton

Alpha Editions

This edition published in 2024

ISBN 9789362517203

Design and Setting By
Alpha Editions
www.alphaedis.com
Email - info@alphaedis.com

As per information held with us this book is in Public Domain.
This book is a reproduction of an important historical work.
Alpha Editions uses the best technology to reproduce historical work
in the same manner it was first published to preserve its original nature.
Any marks or number seen are left intentionally to preserve.

Contents

CHAPTER I.	- 1 -
CHAPTER II.	- 6 -
CHAPTER III.	- 12 -
CHAPTER IV.	- 18 -
CHAPTER V.	- 27 -
CHAPTER VI.	- 36 -
CHAPTER VII.	- 44 -
CHAPTER VIII.	- 50 -
CHAPTER IX.	- 59 -
CHAPTER X.	- 64 -
CHAPTER XI.	- 68 -
CHAPTER XII.	- 77 -
CHAPTER XIII.	- 83 -
CHAPTER XIV.	- 88 -

CHAPTER I.

Brother and Sister—Forebodings—Nettleton.

War! Oh! how much of misery is expressed in that one word! It tells its own tale of woe, of blood, of broken hearts and desolated homes, of hopes blighted, of poverty and crime, of plunder, peculation and official tyranny, of murder and sudden death. In short, it develops all the baser passions of the human heart, changing a peaceful world to a world of woe, over which the destroying angel well might weep.

Come, oh, thou angel, Peace!

The "Army of the Mississippi," as it was termed, had been unsuccessful in their pursuit of the rebel General Price. A portion of it, or rather the division commanded by General Sigel, had advanced from Springfield, Missouri, upon the Wilson creek road, as far as the famous battle-ground rendered immortal by the death of General Lyon, but finding no enemy, it had encamped upon Grand Prairie, a few miles to the west of the bloody field. All in camp was upon the "tip-toe of expectation." The lovely scene spread out before the view, was sufficient to inspire the heart of man to great and glorious deeds. The broad, rolling prairie lay there, like heaven's great carpet. The long grass waved in the breeze, presenting the appearance of a deep-green sea, undulating in low swells as if Queen Mab's wand were wafting over it; the autumn's frost had changed thousands of the delicate emerald blades to purple, yellow, and scarlet, while, intermixed with these, was the white prairie flower, lending to the scene an almost fairy-like aspect. The large "Fremont" tents were arranged in rows, in a tasty manner; flags were flying; bands were discoursing sweet strains which echoed far and wide; squads of soldiers in vari-colored uniforms were lounging lazily on the grass, while those detailed for mess or guard duty, were busily prosecuting their assigned tasks. To the east of the camp appeared a wall of forest-kings, their verdure, also, touched by the frost, presenting a variety of colors, and glistening in the sunlight.

Few in that small army had witnessed the horrors of the battle-field; but, like all "green" troops, conceiving that there was much of romance connected with the deadly field, and that heroes were created by a single brave deed, the mass of Sigel's men were eager to meet the foe. It had been given out that the entire army was to join this division on the prairies, and that an advance was to be made at once against Price, who was then at Cassville, some forty miles distant, to the southward.

"I think we can safely count upon a desperate battle by the day after to-morrow," exclaimed one of a party of five, seated within a captain's tent—

four of whom were at a table, with cups and wine before them. The fifth person was making himself generally useful, acting in the capacity of a servant.

"You have fleshed your maiden sword at Springfield, and I did not suppose you would be anxious for another fight. I confess I can not gaze upon such scenes without a shudder, and, if duty would permit, I would willingly sheathe my sword forever."

"Captain Hayward, you are low-spirited to-day," answered the first speaker.

"I am, indeed, Lieutenant Wells. And can you wonder? My sister is here!"

"I only wish mine was!"

"That is a rash wish, my friend. She would be exposed to much danger, and I never want mine to gaze upon a battle-field. No! where *men* cut each other's throats, delicate, sensitive women should not be near!"

"Could you find no way in which to send her from Springfield to St. Louis?" asked Wells.

"I could have done so by the mail coach but, you know, the entire distance of one hundred and thirty miles, from Springfield to Rolla, or to Tipton upon the other route, is infested with guerrillas, and I feared to send her. I preferred she should brave the dangers of the camp or even the battle-field with me."

Captain Hayward bent his head upon his hands and was silent. It was some moments before any one ventured to speak. All appeared to be oppressed with a strange sadness. At length one of the party, Captain Gilbert, slapping him familiarly upon the shoulder, and endeavoring to speak gayly, said:

"Come, come, Harry, this won't do! you must shake off every vestige of blues. You are suffering still from the wound you received in the Warsaw skirmish, and it makes you low-spirited. No doubt your sister will be perfectly safe, and I know she had much rather be with you, to assist you should you need her aid, than to be safe in St. Louis, enduring the tortures of suspense."

Hayward made no reply. At this moment, a female, delicate and fair, came tripping lightly into the tent, her face wreathed in smiles, and her eyes sparkling with delight; but, as she caught sight of Hayward, she paused, and gazed upon him for a moment, exhibiting the most intense interest; then advancing, and placing her hand upon his shoulder, she spoke:

"Brother!"

Hayward started, and clasping her in his arms, he pressed her close to his heart for a moment. But, gazing into his eyes, she asked:

"What is the matter, dear Harry, you appear ill?"

The countenance of Hayward underwent an instant change, as he replied:

"Not ill, but somewhat depressed in spirits, perhaps, in view of what a day may bring forth."

"Oh! Harry," she said, "I hear there is going to be another fight. Will *you* have to go into it and leave me?"

"Should there be a battle, I shall endeavor to protect you, dear sister."

"But, you will be in danger; perhaps wounded—perhaps killed! Oh! what *would* I do, then? Don't go, Harry!" and the gentle girl threw her arms around her brother's neck and wept. After a moment, he raised her, and pressing his lips to her forehead, said:

"I wish to speak with these gentlemen a moment. Go to your friend Alibamo's tent. I will come for you, soon!" The sister cast back a look of fond solicitude, and left the tent.

Hayward gazed after her a moment, muttering audibly:

"Poor child, what *would* you do if I should fall. You would indeed be alone!"

"Now, captain, I don't think that's half fair," exclaimed the one spoken of as being the servant. "Do you think I am such a darn skunk as to—if you was killed—the darn—not to fight for my capt'n's sister—the skunk—no, I mean, if you die—if she—darn me, if I don't—I—I—" and the speaker, as if unable to express what he *did* mean, suddenly left the tent. All present smiled broadly, and good-humor was thus, for the moment, infused in all hearts.

"Nettleton had a sudden call!" said one.

"He has gone to the sutler for a dictionary!" added another.

"His heart is in the right place," remarked Hayward.

"That's so!" responded all, with emphasis.

"You are safe, with such a 'darn skunk' for your body-guard, Captain Hayward," Gilbert declared, with comic seriousness.

William Nettleton was in height about six feet. His general appearance was very singular. His hair was nearly white—naturally so; his eyes of a light green and large; his carriage very loose—indeed, when he walked, one would almost expect to see him fall in pieces. His feet were huge in dimensions. He had the appearance of a half-witted, illy-formed person; but he was, withal, neither one nor the other. Having been detached from the company to which he belonged, to act as servant to Captain Hayward, he soon became so greatly attached and devoted to the captain, as to be styled his "body-guard." This attachment was not fictitious, nor did it proceed from a spirit of military sycophancy or subserviency; it was felt. Nettleton had evinced more than ordinary courage on several occasions, and had, also, displayed so much judgment with his intrepidity, that he had received offers of advancement; but these he declined, preferring, as he expressed himself, "to stay with my capt'n, the first what promoted me."

It will also be well to explain the presence of ladies in the camp. Miss Mamie Hayward was the sister of Captain Hayward, who, having received intelligence that her brother was wounded, had visited Springfield for the purpose of ministering to his wants. At the time of her arrival Fremont's "Army of the Mississippi" was marching upon that place, and the journey from Rolla or Tipton was safe. But soon, those roads were infested with guerrillas, and, as they were poorly guarded, it was not thought prudent that the ladies who had reached Springfield should attempt a return. Miss Hayward, therefore, remained with her brother. This same reason will apply to all the ladies in camp, of which there were several—conspicuous among whom was the wife of Adjutant Hinton, one of the officers of the well-known "Benton Cadets." She was usually addressed as "Alibamo"—her name when a captive in Price's hands. She was very beautiful, and of that daring, determined nature which has immortalized so many women of the West. In company with Alibamo, was a young lady who acted in the capacity of waiting-maid, but who really appeared more like a companion. This female possessed the not particularly euphonious name of Sally Long.

"I must join with Nettleton in my reproaches, Captain Hayward," answered Lieutenant Wells, in a subdued tone. "You forget my conversation with you last night!"

"No, Wells. You informed me of your affection for my sister, but you have never addressed her as a lover. How do you know that she will return your love? If she could return it, I confess, lieutenant, I do not know any one to whom I would more willingly see her united; but, if she can not, how could you assume to become her protector?"

"If such should be the case, and the fortunes of war should deprive her of a brother, rest assured that, not only myself, but every man in camp would willingly shed his blood in her defense, and care for her as a sister!"

"Thank you. I *do* feel a foreboding of evil. I believe I shall be killed in the coming battle. If this should be the case, I commend her to your care. But, my nerves are excited. I will walk into the open air. No! I would be alone!" he added, as one of the officers arose as if to accompany him.

As he left the tent one of the party, a Captain Walker, exclaimed:

"Well, I hope things are all right, but I have my doubts!"

"Your doubts of what?" asked Wells.

"Humph! well, no matter. *You* are too directly interested to listen to the explanation. But, perhaps you will find out some day."

"Do you intend, sir, to cast any slur upon Captain Hayward?"

Captain Walker did not reply, but left the tent. An hour or more had passed, and Hayward did not return. It was now quite dark, when suddenly the assembly was sounded, and, all anxious, the troops fell in. The order was read:

"Pack knapsacks, and have every thing in readiness for a move at daylight."

All was excitement, and every preparation was made for a forward movement. But soon it began to be whispered that the orders were to return. In a short time it was officially announced that the movement was, in reality, *back to Springfield*, and from thence to Rolla and St. Louis. Many were the expressions of disappointment and regret, and some even ventured to denounce the policy. Fremont had been superseded in the field, and General Hunter, his successor, had abandoned the campaign, then on the very eve of its final consummation.

CHAPTER II.

The Tragedy of the Stream. Who was Guilty?

When Captain Hayward left the tent, he proceeded to the stream which skirted the woods. Bending over it, he bathed his fevered brow. Then he seated himself upon the bank of the river, and, resting his head upon his hands, was, for a long time, absorbed in his thoughts. A human form flitted lightly past. Hayward raised his head and listened, but all was quiet again, and, in the darkness of the night he could distinguish nothing.

"I was mistaken!" he said to himself. "If I was not, and a human being is around, I will wager it was Nettleton, who, anxious for my safety, has followed me."

The captain was again silent for a moment, when the breaking of a twig betrayed the presence of some person. Hayward raised his head and called:

"William! William Nettleton!"

"Sir!" answered a voice but a few feet from the captain.

"Why did you follow me, William?"

"Cos I'm a darn skunk," drawled the person addressed, as he emerged out of the darkness. "And——*Curse you!*"

The person speaking was before him. In an instant Hayward sprung to his feet, but, with a cry of agony exclaimed: "Great God, Nettleton—why have you—oh God, save me—you've killed me—I die!" And, falling heavily forward, the words died upon his tongue.

The murderer bent over the murdered for a moment; then, with some haste, rolled the body into the water, and turned from the spot. He paused under the shade of a tree, and listened for the tread of a sentry, that he might enter the camp unobserved. With a half-suppressed laugh he uttered his thoughts:

"I have done it, sure; and now that it is done, I must progress—no retreating now. I think I'll win. Good-by, captain, and give my respects to my friends as you float downstream."

He proceeded with caution toward the camp, and was soon lost in the city of canvas.

The tattoo soon sounded. Lights were extinguished, and all was quiet, save in a few tents, which appeared to be those of officers. Yet, there were aching hearts within that camp, and, as the night progressed, many were the anxious inquiries as to why Captain Hayward did not return.

In a large tent, near that occupied by Captain Hayward, were seated three ladies. One was Miss Hayward; another was Alibamo, or, as she is now a wife, she should be called Mrs. Adjutant Hinton; the other was Miss Sally Long, the waiting-maid of Alibamo. Before this tent paced a special guard; beside it was a tent of much smaller dimensions, occupied by Nettleton and *his* servant, black George, or, as Nettleton used to call him, "Swasey's nigger."

"I fear something has befallen my brother. He does not return, and it is now twelve o'clock!"

"Don't be alarmed," said Alibamo, in a soothing voice; "your brother is most likely at the head-quarters of General Sigel. He may be detained on business. Come, let us retire."

"No, not while my brother is absent."

At this moment the guard came to the tent entrance and said:

"Ladies, if you have not yet retired Captain Walker requests the pleasure of a few words with Miss Hayward."

"Oh, Alibamo, I fear that man; he looks at me so strangely. But perhaps he brings news of my brother. I will see him. Bid the captain enter."

As Walker entered he appeared agitated, but controlling his emotions, he said:

"Ladies, you will pray excuse me. I feel that I *must* speak now, as it may be my last opportunity. We—or, I should say the army—will be separated at Springfield, and I shall see you no more."

"Do you bring news of my brother?" asked Miss Hayward.

"No! His disappearance is very strange. But I came to speak of myself."

"What would you say?"

"This, Miss Hayward. I have loved you long and dearly. To-morrow we may be parted, and I would ask you, should the fortunes, or rather the misfortunes, of war deprive you of a brother's love and protection, will you not permit me to seek you out and become your future protector?"

"Captain Walker, these words surprise me, and I think propriety demanded that they should have been spoken in the presence of my brother."

"Pardon me, dear lady. I have waited until this hour for your brother's return, and at last, fearing I should have no other opportunity, I ventured to visit you now. You have a friend and sister in Alibamo, and surely you will not fear to speak before her."

"I can not answer your question—it refers to the future."

"Then for the *present*. Let me speak plainly, and I beg you will do the same. Can you not at least regard me *now* as your friend and protector, and give me a friend's privileges?"

The timid girl turned toward Alibamo, and in an inaudible voice, spoke a word.

"She answers promptly, *no*!" replied Alibamo, somewhat sterner than was her usual manner.

"You *love* another, then?" asked Walker.

Miss Hayward did not reply.

"Is the favored one Lieutenant Wells?" again asked Walker.

"You are impertinent, Captain Walker," replied Alibamo. "I must request you to retire. How can you thus, in her brother's absence, address her in this manner?"

At this moment there was a commotion in the tent of Nettleton. The voice of the negro was heard, exclaiming:

"I he'rd you, massa Nettleton. There ain't no use in you denyin' it. I he'rd massa cap'n say, 'Oh, Nettleton, ye kill me!' Oh Lord, if eber I get out ob *dis* scrape, ye'll neber catch dis chile in such another one."

"Is the nigger crazy? What is the darn skunk talking about?"

"Oh, you needn't make b'lieve ignoramus on dis 'ere question. I he'rd ye."

"Now, look a here, you unconscionable dark; if you have got any thing to say, spit it out. Don't make a darn skunk of yourself."

"Oh! won't I fotch ye up in de morning? Yes, sah!"

"Are you going to speak, and say what you mean?"

"Oh, golly! You go back on de cap'n dat way!"

"What cap'n? Out with it, or I'll break your head and every bone in your body," exclaimed Nettleton, in a state of undisguised excitement.

"Serve dis nigger as ye did de cap'n, and den put his body in de riber!"

The negro had scarcely uttered these words when Nettleton seized him. He set up a terrible howl, which brought Captain Walker to their tent.

"What is all this fuss about?" asked Walker.

The negro went on to explain as follows:

"Why, ye see, massa cap'n, I went ober to dat yar house across de riber, to see Miss Julia, a col'd gal dat used to be my sweetheart. Well, I see'd de Johnnies comin', and I ran down to de riber to come on dis side, but dey come so close to me dat dis chile hid behind a big log. Den dey stop right by me, and say, 'Golly, we can't cotch nobody.' Den I he'rd some one on de oder side ob de riber say, "Oh, Nettleton, you—"

"Silence this stuff! You have been drunk. If you speak upon this subject again, I'll cut your black throat."

"I'se dumb, massa cap'n."

Quiet had now been restored, and all parties retired for the few hours that intervened before morning. But it was evident all were not asleep. Several times a stealthy step was heard, and a shadow flitted past the white canvas tent, dimly seen by the pale starlight.

Morning came at last, and all was astir. Captain Hayward had not yet returned. The inquiry was made if any one had seen him.

"I have not seen him since last evening at twilight," replied Walker, "at which time he acted very strangely, and talked about the injustice of war. I am inclined to think he has deserted and joined the enemy."

"Oh, you darn skunk!" yelled Nettleton, as he sprang forward, and was about to strike the speaker. But, checking himself, he added: "It's well you wear them gilt things on your shoulders, or I'd teach you to call *my* cap'n such names."

"If you would save yourself trouble you had better remain quiet, Nettleton," replied Walker, as he fixed his eyes significantly upon him.

"*I* knows where Cap'n Hayward am," said the negro, stepping forward.

"Where is he?" sobbed Miss Hayward, pressing forward, in her eagerness.

"He is—"

"Silence!" yelled Walker.

"Let him speak," said the colonel. "Go on, George. Where is the captain?"

"Down dar!" The negro trembled violently, and glanced at Nettleton.

"What do you mean?"

"He's in de riber—killed dead, sure!"

A wild shriek rose upon the air as Miss Hayward fell back into the arms of Alibamo, insensible.

"By whom was he killed?"

"By massa Nettleton dar, *sure*. I he'rd across de riber, jis as plain as day."

Nettleton started back in horror, his eyes extending widely, and his frame trembling. A general murmur of disbelief ran through the crowd.

"Did you *see* him do the deed?" asked the colonel.

"Golly, I couldn't see much, it war so dark. But I hear massa cap'n say, 'Oh, Nettleton, you kill me!' Golly, see how massa Nettleton shake!"

"Where was this?"

"Rite down by dat tree. His blood is all ober de ground; I jest see it."

In an instant Nettleton had dashed off for the spot indicated. In accordance with an order from the colonel he was pursued. Reaching the locality named, he gazed upon the ground. It was red with blood—fresh blood. He threw himself upon the earth, and wept and moaned, and called upon his captain to return. His grief was terrible to behold. By this time the officers and many of the men had arrived. They gazed upon the grief-stricken servant with respect, and more than one expression of sympathy was heard.

"If Captain Hayward has been murdered, it was not by that boy. Nettleton loved his captain too much to harm him," said Lieutenant Wells. "I am inclined to think the deed has been done by skulking guerrillas."

"I incline to your opinion, Lieutenant Wells, as to the innocence of Nettleton. But, as to the deed having been done by guerrillas, it is not likely. It is much too near camp."

"But Hayward certainly had no enemy in our camp who would have done this deed."

"We do not know the secret motives which animate the human heart," replied Walker, in a tone and manner not devoid of meaning.

"Let instant search be made for the body," commanded the colonel. It was done, but no trace of it could be found, although the water was too shallow to have permitted it to float down the river. Attention was again directed to Nettleton, who was sitting erect, gazing at a piece of sharp, bloody steel which he held in his hand. Viewing it a moment, he sprung to his feet, and fixed his eyes upon Lieutenant Wells. Then he turned to the colonel and handed him the blade. That officer examined it. Directing his gaze upon Lieutenant Wells, he asked:

"Has any one among you a small Spanish dirk, with a highly-polished and ornamented blade?"

"I *had* such a one," replied Wells, "but I have missed it for several days."

The colonel instantly turned toward the camp, commanding all to follow him. He halted before the tent of Lieutenant Wells, and said:

"You, Captain Walker, and you, Adjutant Hinton, enter this tent, and tell me what you find."

The search lasted but a moment, during which time Wells had been assisting Miss Hayward, but not without evincing much agitation. Walker now appeared, holding in his hand a bowl of bloody water, and exhibiting the broken stiletto, covered with blood, which had been found in the overcoat pocket of Wells. A shirt, also, was found, which was stained with blood.

"What can you say to this damning proof of your guilt?" asked the colonel.

"I know nothing of it."

"Arrest the murderer of Captain Harry Hayward!" commanded the colonel, in a loud voice.

The guards instantly seized him.

"Murderer! *He* a murderer—and of my brother! No! no! This is some dreadful dream. Oh, tell me my brother is not murdered; it will kill me. Oh, see! Pity a friendless girl who kneels to you and begs you to tell her that you have *not* deprived her of a dear brother. Speak to me, Edward. I did love you, and you would not harm him."

Wells could not speak. He had never spoken to Miss Hayward of his love for her; but *now*, in the delirium of her grief, she had confessed her love for him. Oh, what a moment!

Walker advanced to raise Miss Hayward from her bended position before Wells.

"Paws off, ye darn skunk!" yelled Nettleton, as he hurled Walker to the ground. "*I* alone am her protector now."

CHAPTER III.

The Proposal—The Interruption—The Indian—The Rescue—The Wounded Man—The Mystery.

NEAR the village of Ozark, at the base of a ridge of mountains of that name, runs a most beautiful stream or river, which bears the name of the village, and is one of the tributaries of the north fork of the Gasconade. Its banks are high, and covered with a thick but small growth of the "scrub" oak, peculiar to that portion of Missouri. The bed of the river sparkles with brilliant white and yellow pebbles, polished by the rush of waters for thousands of years. A fine bridge spans the stream along the main road, that runs through the only opening in the forest for miles around. After crossing this bridge, and ascending a sharp hill, the village of Ozark is reached. This consists of about twenty ordinary-looking dwellings, a court-house, and a rough building, dignified by the name hotel. Beyond the village, and higher up the mountain, is a line of rolling hills, which overlook the country for miles around. On one of these, and near the edge of a grove, were to be seen a cluster of tents, and, from the number of horses picketed but a short distance away, it would at once be supposed, from a distance, to be a cavalry camp, with, perhaps, a section of artillery.

On a sloping point, extending from the side of the bridge to the stream, and reclining upon the turf, were two persons. The one a young man of marked appearance, and the other a female of much beauty, although her dress bespoke her a native of that portion of the country.

"Nettie, when do you expect your sister to return?"

"It is difficult to answer, Charles, but I trust very soon."

"Have you not heard from her recently?"

"No. There is no way in which she can communicate with me. The mails have been discontinued, you are aware, from Rolla to Springfield."

"If you can *visit* the army, I presume you can both dispatch and receive letters. Are you not very anxious to learn how she is treated among the Federals?"

"I am most anxious; still I have no fears."

"I can not feel as you do upon that subject. I would not awaken useless fears in your breast, but *I* have not so much confidence in their magnanimous natures."

"Charles, you told me to-day for the first time, that you loved me, and asked me if I could not address you as *dear* Charles. You have been very kind to me, and, on one occasion, you rescued me from the hands of a villain. I feel grateful—truly so. But, whatever my feelings may be, I never can wed my country's enemy. Look yonder. You see that white cottage. Once it was beautifully adorned with creeping vines, and the lawn before it bloomed with flowers and shrubbery. But, dearer than all, within its walls lived my father and my sister. Look at it now! Its beauty has departed—it is a *wreck*; father and sister have been driven from it, while I have been detained here by *force*. You profess to love me. If you do so, *prove it*! We are now more than a mile from the rebel camp, and you can escape with me to Springfield."

"I will assist *you* to escape; indeed, I will accompany you a portion of the way to Springfield. But *I* must return to my own people and fight with them to the last. I *do* love you, and I *would* become your husband, gladly, if I could be satisfied you loved me for myself alone. But, I can not sacrifice one jot of honor or principle to win even you, dear Nettie."

"And you will go with me, now?"

"Yes—stay, what is that? Did you not hear a low, moaning sound?"

"I heard nothing."

"Well, perhaps I am mistaken. But I fancied I heard such a sound. No matter. I will go with you now to Springfield."

"To what purpose, young man?"

The speaker was a powerful person, and had emerged from the bridge just in time to hear the last sentence of Charles Campbell.

"So, sir," he continued, "you would desert us, and join the Yankees, and all for your foolish regard for this vixen!"

"Colonel Price, if you were not an officer I would make you *eat* your words. I have served you faithfully, and you have no right to question my loyalty. I do *not* intend to desert, neither is this lady a *vixen* any more than you are a *coward*."

Price started, bit his lips, and frowned fiercely. At length he asked:

"Why did you propose visiting Springfield with this——lady?"

"I intended to accompany her a portion of the way, and then to return to my duty."

"Why does *she* wish to visit Springfield?"

"Because her father and sister are both in St. Louis, and she wishes to rejoin them."

"Did not yonder cottage belong to her father?"

"It did."

"He was one of the most bitter opposers in this section. And you love his abolition daughter?"

"I love his *daughter*, sir!"

"Enough. You will return to camp this moment. I will take charge of this young lady. When I rejoin you, I shall put your loyalty and your *courage* to the test. Do you see yonder boat?"

He pointed up the river. A small boat was seen floating down the stream, in which three men were sitting erect, and the form of a fourth, lying prostrate.

"How do you propose testing my loyalty, Colonel Price?"

"That boat contains a Yankee officer. He is to be hung up by the neck. You shall perform the job."

"Is not that man *wounded*, Colonel Price?"

"Yes, very badly so, I am informed."

"*Then I will not perform the base thing you propose.*"

Price drew a revolver, and pointing it to the head of Campbell, commanded him to start at once for camp. He had scarcely done so, when a powerful Indian sprung from concealment, and snatched the weapon from his hand. At the same time he seized Price, as if he had been a child, and hurled him into the water below. Without waiting to watch the result of this sudden immersion upon the chivalrous colonel, he caught the maiden in his arms, and bounded off in the direction of Springfield. As he started, he beckoned to the young man and muttered:

"Come—follow—me save her!"

Price floundered about in the water for a moment, and finally succeeded in reaching the shore just as the boat came up.

"Come—quick—join me in the pursuit!" yelled Price.

The three men leaped upon the bank, and, at the command of Price, all discharged their pieces after the retreating Indian, but without effect. Pursuit was then ordered, but Price, observing that Campbell did not follow, turned and asked:

"Are *you* not coming, sir?"

"No!" was the prompt reply.

Price felt for his revolver, but finding it gone, he only muttered, "Curse you," and then commenced the pursuit. For over a mile it was kept up. The pursuers gained upon the Indian, who was considerably obstructed in his flight by the weight of the female. At last Price exclaimed:

"By the eternal, there come the Yankees!"

Sure enough, just appearing in view upon an elevated point a little beyond, was seen a squadron of cavalry, and a section of flying artillery rapidly advancing.

"To the hill! Give the signal for our guns—to the bridge—secure the prisoner in the boat!"

These commands were given by Price, as he commenced a rapid retreat toward the bridge. Pausing on the hill just before reaching it, he unfurled a small flag and made a signal. In an instant all was astir in the rebel camp, and artillery and cavalry soon came dashing down the hill.

"Where is the prisoner?" yelled Price, as he came to the bridge.

"Perhaps the young man you left here has taken him to camp."

"But the boat is gone! However, there is no time to be lost, now. They are upon us! Quick!"

Colonel Price started for the opposite end of the bridge, followed by his three confederates. The rebel troops were still some distance from that end of the bridge nearest their camp, which it was evident they intended reaching, if possible, in order to sweep the narrow passage, if the Union forces attempted to cross. The Federals, however, were the first to gain that point. But, had a crossing been effected, as soon as they reached the opposite side they would have been exposed to the most galling fire of the enemy, as there was a large space of flat, swampy ground in front; and then a sharp bluff, upon which the rebel artillery would, in such a case, be planted. The commander of the Federals, observing this situation at a glance, ordered a halt, and brought his section of artillery into position. One piece was placed so as to enfilade the bridge, and the other upon a little rise of ground, in a position where it could sweep their lines beyond. The rebels observing this, threw forward two guns, amid a deadly fire from the Unionists, and succeeded in taking a position upon the opposite end of the bridge. Several rounds of grape were hurled back and forth, but as the cover was good, but little damage was done. The cavalry attempted a crossing, but the thick growth of oaks prevented. A charge was about to be ordered across the bridge, when an explosion took place, and it was shattered to fragments. Taking advantage of this, the rebels made a rapid flight. As pursuit was useless, the command was given to fall back to Springfield.

The Indian we have spoken of now approached the commander, leading the trembling woman, and said:

"Me save—you save—white squaw!"

"Do you require my protection?" asked the commander.

Nettie told her story in an artless manner, of which the reader has gleaned all necessary particulars. She was kindly provided for, and soon reached Springfield in perfect safety.

Soon after the arrival, a soldier came to the tent of the commanding officer, presenting a bit of paper.

"Colonel, I picked up this scrap near the bridge, but did not look at it until this moment. It may be of importance."

The colonel took the paper and read aloud:

"A suspicion of my fidelity to the Confederate cause has crossed the mind of my commanding officer, Lieutenant-Colonel A. M. Price, simply because I consented to assist Miss Nettie Morton to reach Springfield, from which point she might be able to rejoin her friends, who formerly resided in Ozark, but are now in St. Louis. I was condemned, in consequence, to be the executioner of a *wounded* Federal officer. At this cowardly act my whole nature revolted. Chance has favored me, and I have determined to save him. In what manner I can not here write, fearing this paper should fall into Confederate hands, and my plans be thus interrupted. I can not learn who he is. I asked his name, and I have some reason to believe that Miss Morton may throw some light upon the subject, as the only words he spoke were 'Net—murdered—sister—.' He bore the rank of captain.

CHARLES CAMPBELL."

The colonel turned toward Miss Morton, who was seated in his tent, and asked:

"Do you feel any *especial* interest in any Union officer now with us?"

Miss Morton hung her head and blushed.

"Do not fear to speak, and frankly, too, Miss Morton. Perhaps the welfare of one you love—perhaps his safety, may depend upon your candid confession."

"I—I—"

"Have you ever *met* one of our officers?"

"But once. And then I only passed the evening in his society. He was kind, but he has forgotten me!"

"It is enough, you love him. But the short time he was with you could scarcely have made an impression so deep that he would mutter your name in his delirium. And yet, the wounded man was near your residence. And he exclaimed 'Net—'. Your name is Nettie, is it not?"

"It is."

"And what is the name of him you refer to?"

"Captain HARRY HAYWARD!"

The officer was visibly affected. "'Nettie.' 'Net—.' 'Nettleton!' *'Murdered.'* 'Sister.' It is very strange. Harry Hayward's body was not found, but he was assassinated. Ah, I begin to fathom the mystery." He murmured all this in words not audible to the astonished Miss Morton, and left the tent slowly, as if oppressed with the weight of a momentous thought.

CHAPTER IV.

Nettleton's Adventure in a Noose—Some Important Information.

THE surprise of Walker was very great at the unexpected movement of Nettleton. His sword flashed from its scabbard, and he made a half-pass at his breast. But, checking himself, he said:

"William, I can forgive you in consideration of your grief, and I spare you, that you may assist in the care of Miss Hayward. Curse him!" he muttered to himself, "I would strike the infernal dog dead at my feet, but the act would only place a greater barrier between me and my prize. Miss Hayward," he added aloud, "you will always find me ready and most anxious to serve you."

"Miss Hayward will not lack for friends, sir!" replied Alibamo, in a tone of contempt.

"Captain Walker, I shall place the prisoner in your charge. You will forward at once." These words were spoken by the colonel.

Walker bit his lip, and was silent. He then commanded the guard to forward, muttering as he did so:

"The second most agreeable job. I'll revenge myself upon him."

As the guard formed around Lieutenant Wells, he turned to Miss Hayward, and said:

"Oh! dear lady, you have inadvertently confessed that you had some regard for me. This is not a time to speak of such things, but I will now say to you, that which has never before passed my lips, excepting to your brother. I love you, with a devotion, ardent as it is pure and holy; and by that love I swear, and beg you to believe, that I have never harmed your brother!"

Miss Hayward turned toward him, and made a movement as if to reach his side, but Walker held aloft the bloody knife, which met her gaze, and, with a shudder, she turned to Alibamo.

"Forward!" cried Walker, and Edward Wells, the once popular officer and general favorite, was urged on, bound and guarded, charged with, and generally believed guilty of, the foulest of crimes. But yesterday he was on the road to honor and fame; now he was marching forward to a disgraceful death. The entire division was soon in motion.

Nettleton now approached Miss Hayward, and said:

"Miss Mamie, I am going to do all for you such a darn sk— I mean such a chap as me *can* do; but, I'm feard that ain't much. But you're going now where there ain't no danger, and if you please, I'm a going to stay behind and hunt for the captain."

"Oh! thank you, William," sobbed Miss Hayward. "How can I ever repay you, dear friend?"

"Don't—don't!" said William. A choking sensation came over him, and, unable to say more, he turned away, only to be comforted by Miss Sally Long, who placed her hands upon his shoulders, and said:

"William, if you will find the captain, I'll *love you dearly*!"

Nettleton started back, opened his eyes wide—so he did his mouth, as if attempting to speak. His lower jaw wagged two or three times, but no sound was heard. Then turning his eyes, he saw the gaze of all fixed upon him, and started off suddenly upon a run, exclaiming as he did so:

"Who ever thought it possible that *I* should ever be loved by Sally—such a darn skunk—a sweet gal, I mean!"

Nettleton did not pause until he had overtaken the colonel, of whom he requested permission to remain and make a more thorough search for his captain.

"No, William," was the reply. "We will not be a mile distant before the enemy's scouts will be here, and you will be taken prisoner."

"No fear, they don't notice such as me!"

"But your uniform will be sufficient."

"Oh! I always go prepared. I have another suit *under* this, one as I got from the bushwhack I laid out the other night, as he came noseing around Captain Hayward's tramping ground, and I shall put that on top."

"Well, do as you like, but be careful!"

Nettleton waited for no other words, but turning, proceeded at once to the spot where Hayward received the fatal stab. He sat down for a time, silent and mournful, gazing into the water. He then commenced a scrutinizing search. He became satisfied that the body could not have floated down the river, on account of the shallowness of the water. He crossed the stream, searched upon the opposite bank, and there found the footprints of a number of men. He followed the tracks, and found that *two* persons had descended *into* the river, and out again, near the same spot. He took the measurement of each impression in the mud, and then exclaimed:

"I'll be darned if Lieutenant Wells' boot made any of *them* marks! I know how it is. Captain must have come here last night to think, and some of them darn rebel skunks come up behind him suddenly, and killed him, and then two of them crossed over and got his body, and brought it back, and that accounts for the tracks in and out of the water. But what did they want with him if he was dead? Perhaps he wasn't quite killed, and they took him prisoner. I'll follow these tracks, anyway."

Nettleton followed up the footmarks until they merged into the turnpike, which was so cut up with travel as to prevent him tracing them further. He now returned to the fatal spot. Bending down he examined the earth, still red with blood. Something appeared to interest him, and creeping on his knees, he followed a footprint to the edge of the stream. Here was an impression of *two* boots, side by side, in the mud. Nettleton gazed upon them for a few moments. His breast heaved violently—he clenched his hands, and at last said:

"I've blacked *them* boots. I know 'em well—there is the impression of the *two hearts* in the mud, and there ain't but one pair of boots in our camp as has *two hearts* made with nails in the ball of each boot. Oh, you darn—"

Something caught the eye of Nettleton in the water. He sprung in and secured it. It proved to be a handkerchief, which bore a name upon the corner. He gazed upon it a moment, and said:

"The man as had on *them* boots stood in *them* tracks, and washed himself in that river. He wiped upon this hankercher and then threw it into the water. Folks as washes the evidence of murder off their hands, don't wash in the river, throw away the wiper, and then take a tin pot of bloody water to—"

"What the devil are you doing here?"

Nettleton turned to behold a party of six horsemen who had suddenly approached him. In his anxiety he had forgotten to change his clothing—that is, to cover his blue uniform with the rough gray suit he wore underneath.

"So, you are a Yankee soldier," exclaimed one of the party.

"No I ain't; I'm a darn skunk."

This reply, and the ungainly appearance of Nettleton, caused a laugh throughout the entire party.

"You are not a Yankee soldier? Then what are you doing with that uniform?"

Nettleton looked at his dress, and for the first time became conscious that he had not changed it. He, however, instantly replied:

"I am a spy for the General."

"What General?"

"General Price, to be sure."

This created another fit of merriment.

"Just as if the likes of you would be employed as a spy! Why, you don't know enough to last you half a mile."

"That's just the reason why I *am* a spy. I am such a darn skunk no one pays any attention to me."

"Have you been in the Yankee camp here?"

"Yes."

"Have you a Confederate uniform under that blue?"

"Yes," replied Nettleton, throwing off his coat and exposing the gray.

"To what company and regiment do you belong?"

"No company. I go it on my own hook."

"You know General Price?"

"Yes, very well."

"Have you ever been in his camp?"

"Often."

"Describe him."

Nettleton had, on one occasion, accompanied a party of disguised Union officers into the very camp of Price, while that General held possession of the upper Osage. One of the officers being detected and wounded, was borne along with the retreating rebel army from the Osage to Springfield, and Nettleton had followed on for the purpose of rendering assistance if possible. His apparent stupidity prevented suspicion, and he had been one of the leading spirits in a rescue which afterward occurred. He was, in consequence, not only known to General Price himself, but to a large number of his officers and men, and hence it was very desirable for him to avoid the main army. He supposed that he could deceive his captors, or effect his escape. And the shadowy thought that Captain Hayward might have been seized and borne toward the rebel quarters at once decided his course. He gave an accurate description of Price.

"Good!" answered one of the party, "it is evident you *are* a spy. I find you on the spot the Yankees have just left. You have *their* uniform on and *ours* under it. So far that *looks* well. You know and have perfectly described our General. That renders it certain you have seen him. Now, one of two things is certain: you are a *Yankee* spy, and have been in our camps with that gray uniform *outside*, and then communicated your information to *your* General, or you are a *Confederate* spy, who, having just been in the Yankee camp, must have important information for *our* General. In either case we shall conduct you to him. If you are his man, then all will be right. If you are *not*, then you will be hung within half an hour after your arrival. You understand?"

"I first thought of going on to Springfield, but I think I have all the information necessary, and I had made up my mind to return. I halted here a moment to change my dress; and to look for a Yankee officer who was supposed to be killed last night. But I think he was only badly wounded, and may yet be found alive in the tall grass. Look for him." These words were spoken by Nettleton in an apparently cheerful tone.

"Oh! you mean the captain who was stabbed last night."

"Yes, yes; do you know any thing of him?"

"You appear especially anxious, Mr. What's-your-name?"

"I am anxious," replied Nettleton, fiercely. "He insulted me, and I would be revenged."

"Don't trouble yourself. He'll catch it soon enough. He was *not* killed, but was taken out of the water by us."

"Who struck the blow?" yelled Nettleton.

"No one of our party. We were concealed upon the opposite bank. We could not see the murderer strike, for it was too dark; but we saw the body thrown in the stream, and saw the stabber wash himself in the river. We would have fired upon him, but were afraid of rousing the Yanks. We waited until he left the body, after throwing it into the stream, and then we recovered it. The man was still alive. He had only fainted from loss of blood. We dressed his wound as well as we could, and then conveyed him to a house the other side of the pike. He will recover; but Colonel Price has an especial spite against him. He met him once at Springfield. So, *when* he recovers he will be hung."

"Where is he now?" asked Nettleton.

"At a little house not fifty rods from here, just the other side of the pike."

Without a word, Nettleton bounded like a deer in the direction the Federal forces had taken. But a dozen shots were fired after him, and he fell. He was soon secured, when it was ascertained that one bullet had cut the neck badly, and another had struck the ankle, although it had not broken the bone. He was still able to walk, and, after being bound, he was dragged forward toward Cassville.

A march of forty miles was almost too much even for the tough Nettleton, more especially as he had received a severe shot in the ankle; but he bore up firmly, and at last arrived at the outskirts of the rebel camp. He had become very lame, and rolled about like a ship in a heavy sea. As he entered the camp, many were the jeers and taunts which hailed this specimen of the Yankee soldier. Nettleton made no reply, although his countenance bespoke his contempt.

He was now near the quarters of Price.

"By thunder!" yelled one of the Confederate soldiers, "that is the very fellow who fooled us at Springfield. Hang him! Hang him!"

An explanation was soon made, and Nettleton's fate appeared certain, as a "drumhead" court-martial had already been convened. Sentence was soon given—the Yankee spy was to be hung upon the spot!

A rough scaffolding was formed, under a large tree, and a rope, with the fatal noose attached, thrown over a limb. Nettleton ascended the platform in silence, although his frame trembled.

"I never saw a Yankee yet that did not fear to die," exclaimed one of the bystanders.

"Then you see one now, you darn skunk," replied Nettleton.

"Why do you tremble, then?" asked the Confederate.

"I was thinking of the captain, and of his poor sister 'Mamie.'"

"Ha! ha! ha! This booby is in love. A romantic spy. And the idol of his passion is called 'Mamie!'"

"You lie, you dog!" yelled Nettleton. "I only—"

"What is all this?" asked a stately-looking officer, who had just approached, and before whom all the rest fell back.

"A spy, General," was the response.

"Why was he not brought to *my* quarters?"

"Because Raines ordered a drumhead court-martial."

"Release the man until I have conversed with him."

Nettleton was released, and, as he descended from the scaffolding, he was recognized by General Price.

"We have met before?" asked Price.

"Yes, General, we have," was the prompt reply of Nettleton.

"What were you doing in my camp the *first* time we met?"

"Serving my captain, whom I love."

"Good! What are you doing here now?"

"That will require considerable explanation," added Nettleton.

"Go on," said Price.

"Well, General, some darn skunk *murdered* my captain, and when our troops left Grand Prairie, on their return to Springfield, I remained behind to search for his body. I am *no* spy."

"But you said you were a spy, serving General Price," replied one of the soldiers who had brought Nettleton to the rebel camp.

"How can you explain this?" asked Price.

"Well, ye see, General, Miss Sally—no, I mean Miss Mamie—that's the captain's sister—will break her poor heart and die of grief if she can't learn something about her brother. Them darn skunks as arrested me told me that Captain Hayward was *not* killed. Besides this, as nice a darn sk— I mean as good a man as ever lived, and one who loves Miss Sally—no—that Miss Sally keeps running in my head—one as loves Miss Mamie, is accused of murdering the captain. But I know better, for I found proof enough to convict the right one. I wanted to tell Mamie that Sally—darn Sally—that her brother was *not* dead, and to clear Lieutenant Wells and convict the one as did the deed. So I told them sneaks as how I *was* a spy, in hopes they'd let me alone."

"Would you give any information you may have gleaned here, if I should set you free?"

"I ain't no such darn skunk, General. Honor is honor bright with me."

"What have you seen here?"

"A lot of the darndest sapheads I ever met."

"If I should set you free, will you fight against me?"

"Like the devil, the first time we meet in fair play."

"Why do you wear that gray suit under your uniform?"

"Because captain's always getting himself into some scrape, and I have to hunt him up. Sometimes I have to go among the Johnnies to do it, and then the blue ain't healthy."

"Will you ever act as spy upon me if I let you go?"

"Not unless capt'n does. But I'm his body-guard, and shall go everywhere he does, if I can."

"What is your name?"

"William Nettleton."

"Well, William, I think we shall be obliged to hang you."

"All right, General," answered Nettleton, stepping upon the scaffolding again. "And them darn sneaks shan't say they never see'd a Yankee die bravely. But, General, let me ask of you one favor. You don't want to see a good fellow shot for what he didn't do, and a murderer go clear, do you?"

"Certainly not."

"Then all I ask is, that you send this handkerchief to Colonel Mann, and tell him the murderer didn't wash in a basin in his tent, but in the river, and then threw this wiper away; and that the guilty one has *two hearts*, made with nails, on the sole of each boot. And tell Sally—no, Mamie—that the captain is—Lieutenant Wells—and Walker—the skunk, when I'm dead—that Sally—no, capt'n, won't think of poor Nettleton—and—"

"Oh stop! stop! William, I can never recollect all this. You had better go yourself and attend to this matter."

"What, General? Do you mean it?" cried William, as he sprung from the scaffold and gazed earnestly at Price.

"On one condition I will permit you to go."

"Well, what is it?"

"That as soon as you have given your evidence in the court-martial which will probably be ordered, you will return at once *and be hung*."

"I'll do it; I'm a loafer if I don't."

"You swear it?"

"Yes, by the great jumping jingo, and Sally Long's tearful eyes!"

"The guard will see this man safely beyond our lines," said Price, speaking to one of his officers, "and furnish him a pass and a horse. Let one of our men accompany him near to the Federal lines, and bring back the animal which William will ride."

Nettleton rushed forward, and grasping the hand of Price, shook it violently, and then exclaimed, as he took his leave:

"General Price, you ain't such a darn sneak as I thought you was!"

CHAPTER V.

The Court-martial and the Hostage.

THE division which had been encamped on Grand Prairie reached Springfield in safety, and formed their temporary camp in the field, back of the brick school-house, which stands about a quarter of a mile to the west of the new court-house.

The first order issued to the officers of the battalion of Benton Cadets, the Thirty-fifth and Thirty-seventh Illinois, was to assemble at a given time, to act upon a court-martial, at the quarters of Major D——, Judge-Advocate, to try the case of Lieutenant Edward Wells, charged with willful murder of Harry Hayward, a captain in the service of the United States of America, and attached to the army of the Mississippi, now under command of Major-General Hunter.

It was a sad day! Lieutenant Wells was a favorite with both officers and men of his command. He always had been mild as a female, kind and benevolent—sacrificing his own comfort for the good of the privates in his battalion. True, some said that Wells would not fight bravely—that he ought to have been created a *woman*; but everybody gave him credit for being the kindest of the kind. When first accused, there arose a very bitter feeling against him. Captain Hayward also was a great favorite with the men. He was a stern but kind soldier. When the news of his brutal murder came to the knowledge of his "boys," their first cry was "revenge," and they naturally sought some one on whom to wreak their vengeance. At first Lieutenant Wells narrowly escaped a summary fate, more especially as it was whispered about camp that Wells had become a suitor for the hand of the fair Mamie Hayward, had been *rejected* by her, and spurned by the captain. But in a short time it was given out that Mamie had confessed her affection for Wells, and that Captain Hayward had remarked in the presence of others, that he deemed Wells an honorable man, and would gladly favor his suit. This turned the tide of feeling in favor of the lieutenant, and when the court-martial was convened, nothing but a consciousness of a soldier's duty prevented an open revolt, or at least a most decided and forcible expression of feeling. But, trusting to the judgment of the officers forming the court, the soldiers decided to await the result.

Have our readers ever witnessed a trial by court-martial? It is not like the ordinary court of justice. First, the charge is read, as thus:

"Lieutenant Edward Wells, of Company H, Battalion of B—— C——, is charged with the willful murder of Harry Hayward, a captain in the U. S. army.

"2d.—Specification.—1st. In this, that said Lieutenant Edward Wells, did, on the night of the seventh day of November, 1861, assassinate and murder said," etc.

Following this, in any case of the kind, would be found a list of "specifications," setting forth in detail, all the chief events connected with the crime.

The prisoner was brought to the tent of Major D—— to answer to the charge. He was very pale, yet perfectly composed; and when the question was asked, the ready and firm response was:

"NOT GUILTY!"

The Judge-Advocate, a noble-hearted but just man, informed the prisoner that he was to act, not only as "prosecuting counsel," but as "counsel" for the prisoner, and that he (the Judge-Advocate) must give the prisoner the benefit of any doubt that might arise in his favor.

To those of our readers not familiar with the *modus operandi* of a court-martial, we would give the following information for their benefit:

The doors of the court are closed to all outsiders. The prisoner makes his plea, and retires. The witnesses are brought forward and examined, but no cross-examination is allowed. If a question is to be asked by any of the officers sitting upon the court, it must be reduced to writing, and silently handed to the Judge-Advocate. If he sees fit to put the question, it is done; if not, it is thrown aside.

We will now proceed to a brief summary of the trial.

"Lieutenant Edward Wells, you are charged with the willful murder of Harry Hayward, a captain in the United States service. What is your plea. Guilty, or *not* guilty!"

"Not guilty!" was the decided response.

"Let the first witness be called, George Swasey, colored."

The person familiarly known as "Swasey's nigger" took the stand. When brought forward, he glanced around as if fearful of something, and then asked:

"Is Massa William Nettletum where he can hear dis chile tell de truff?"

"You have nothing to fear from *any* person, if you *do* speak the truth, and *all* the truth," replied Major D.

"Well den, de fact am dis. I went to see my gal. When I cum back, I met de rebs. I hid behind a log. I see'd some one stick a knife in massa cap'n, and I heard him say:

"'Oh! Nettletum, you kill me!'"

All questions were answered in the same spirit, and it became evident that the negro believed Nettleton the real murderer.

The next witness brought upon the stand was Alibamo Hinton. She swore that Nettleton's tent was next to the one she occupied—that he was in attendance upon her and Miss Hayward, by permission of Captain Hayward, and that Nettleton had *not* been out of her presence that night. In the first part of the evening, Nettleton had remained near her door; in the latter part, he had missed his captain, and had prostrated himself on a rug near the tent entrance. She had seen him there *all night*, as she had not slept at all.

Miss Hayward was too much overcome to appear as a witness, and was excused.

The next witness was Captain Hugh Walker.

The feeling of the soldiers, to learn the result of the trial, was intense, and by the time Captain Walker was called to the stand, some twenty or thirty had crept to the edge of the tent, and endeavored to conceal themselves in the tall grass outside, to catch the proceedings. But they were discovered by Walker, who demanded that they should be removed. This was done, and a guard placed outside.

Captain Walker's oath was as follows:

"On the night of the seventh of November, I followed Captain Hayward from his tent. It was at the time gradually becoming dark. My motive in doing so I will explain. As soon as it began to be rumored that we were to meet Price, I observed a change in the conduct of Captain Hayward. He had ever been the center of attraction. His tent was the 'head-quarters' of 'our circle,' drawn thither by the natural gayety of the captain, and the presence there of ladies. But this feeling appeared to forsake him, and on more than one occasion he denounced the war as inhuman. Pardon me; I would not speak against the dead, but I doubted the loyalty of the man, and *not* his courage, and this it was which induced me to follow him.

"I halted beneath a large tree, which stood near the spot where the murder evidently was committed. I saw the captain seat himself upon the bank. At this time it was quite dark, but I saw a shadow approaching. It passed near me, but I failed to discover who it was. I first thought it might be William Nettleton following his master. I listened attentively, however, as the extreme caution of the intruder attracted my attention. In an instant I heard a groan, a heavy fall, and a voice exclaim: 'Oh, William, where are you? Nettleton, I am murdered. WELLS *is the assassin!*'"

A shudder ran through the court. Major D—— dropped his head upon his hand and was silent. The officers whispered together. At last, a written question was handed to the Judge-Advocate, which was promptly asked:

"Captain Walker, why did you not give the alarm, or arrest the murderer yourself?"

"Sir," was the prompt reply, "the sequel will show. It was dark; I could not distinguish the features of any person two yards distant. I feared he might escape if he should discover me. I therefore followed the murderer cautiously, and he entered the tent of Lieutenant Wells. He did not strike a light, but I listened, and heard him washing himself. I kept close watch upon him until morning, to make sure I was not accusing an innocent man. No one entered or left the tent. The one who washed his hands, and left the bloody water, was Lieutenant Edward Wells."

This evidence was conclusive. But no reason could be assigned for the murder, unless it was that Miss Hayward had been heard to say that she never should marry and leave her brother so long as he lived, and it had now become well known that Wells was a suitor for her hand. Still, he was a favorite with the captain, and even on the day of his death Hayward had been heard to say that he believed Wells a man of honor, whose suit he would favor. The only conclusion which could be arrived at was, that Wells believed the love of a sister was too strong to give immediate place to the love of a wife, and he felt that, the brother once removed, he alone would become the object of Miss Hayward's affection. This, though but a flimsy pretext for so awful a crime, was all that any one could offer in the way of a surmise.

The trial was over. But one decision could be given. It soon was rumored about camp that sentence had been passed, and that at four o'clock the next day it would be read to the prisoner, in presence of the whole division.

The night was wearing on. A form, closely enveloped, approached the tent of the commanding General. It proved to be the lady Alibamo.

"What is the will of our 'daughter of the army?'" asked the General, kindly.

"It is that I may visit Lieutenant Wells, and bring him to my tent. I desire that an interview should take place between Miss Hayward and the doomed man."

The General seated himself at his table, and penned a few words, which he handed to Mrs. Hinton. She glanced at the contents, and then falling at the feet of that officer, she seized his hand, and kissing it, sobbingly exclaimed:

"What! *without* his chains? God bless you! God bless—"

"There, there! Go! go! Don't make *me* weep, or I won't forgive you," returned the veteran warrior, as he turned away.

Alibamo left his tent, and in a few minutes entered her own, in company with Lieutenant Wells, now free from all apparent restraint.

When Wells entered the tent, Miss Hayward was kneeling by the side of her camp cot, her face buried in the folds of its coverings. For several moments not a word was spoken, and, as Wells gazed upon the stricken sister, he trembled violently, while a groan of intense anguish escaped him.

Alibamo advanced, and gently touching her companion, said:

"Mamie, my darling, here is *our friend*, Lieutenant Wells."

Miss Hayward did not raise her head, but reached forth her hand toward Wells, which, quickly kneeling by her side, he took, and pressed to his lips.

"Oh, heaven bless you!" he moaned. "*You* do not believe me capable of the dreadful crime with which I am charged?"

Miss Hayward tried to speak, but convulsive sobs choked her utterance.

"No, my ever kind and dear friend," replied Alibamo, "she does *not* believe you guilty. Nor am I satisfied that Captain Hayward has been killed. I am under the impression that he was wounded and taken prisoner by some rebels, who were lurking near our camp."

"You *hope* for the best, and so do I; but have you any grounds for the formation of such an opinion?" asked Wells.

"Yes, and to me the best of evidence. William Nettleton went in search of the captain. If he was killed, William would have found his body before this, and returned to us with the intelligence. His continued absence convinces me that the captain is still alive, and that his faithful friend Nettleton is at this moment following him. It is this hope which gives me fresh courage, and I believe a few days will see you free, and your name as untarnished as it should be. I wished to tell you this, and I also wished Miss Hayward to express to you personally, her confidence in your innocence;

hence, I brought you here. You may leave us now, as my poor friend is too much agitated to converse."

Wells was about to depart in silence, but Miss Hayward for the first time raised her face, and her tearful eyes met his own. He sprung forward, and kneeling before her, pressed his lips to her white forehead, and said:

"That look is worth to me years of happiness. But, you can read my heart *now*. When I am *proved* innocent, then I will speak the words which must not, till then, pass my lips. God bless you!"

He arose to depart, but was met by Captain Walker, who had just entered the tent.

Walker cast a rapid glance around him, and placing his finger upon his lips, enjoined silence upon all. Wells stood, with arms folded, sternly and suspiciously gazing upon him, while Alibamo asked:

"What are your wishes, sir?"

"To serve you and your friend," was the reply, spoken in a low voice, and with apparent hesitation.

"It must be an important service which could render pardonable the fact, sir, of you having, unannounced, and so rudely, intruded upon our privacy," said Mrs. Hinton.

"It *is* an important service. No less than the rescue of——will you be seated?"

The parties seated themselves in silence, when Walker continued:

"You must pardon me if I speak plainly, and directly to the point. It is necessary that I should be brief."

"Proceed, sir."

"Miss Hayward," continued Walker, turning toward the lady, "I must give a few words of explanation to you. I *did* love—*do* love you now. You need not shrink from me. You will, upon hearing my words, understand me better. No man loves without hope, until there arises between him and the one beloved some impassable barrier. The barrier which arose to blast *my* hopes was, your previous love, and the unfortunate circumstance which has made me an unwilling witness against one to whom, as I think, your heart still clings."

"You will please be brief in comment, and come as quickly as possible to the point in question," replied Mrs. Hinton, as she observed the agitation of Miss Hayward.

"I come to the point now. I know Miss Hayward is very unhappy, and I would not add to it. I would save her lover."

"To whom do you refer?" asked Wells, coldly.

"To you, sir," was the prompt reply.

"I can not claim the title you honor me with, in connection with that lady. Besides, she might not thank *you* for such a service."

"Oh, yes! yes!" eagerly replied Miss Hayward, as she gazed upon the speaker.

"Stay one moment, Miss Hayward," answered Wells. "Let us first learn in what manner my deliverance can be effected. Captain Walker, you can proceed."

"You speak very coldly, Lieutenant Wells, to one who comes to offer you service. But, before I proceed, I must exact a promise, that if my proposition is not accepted, those to whom my words are addressed will make no exposure of the same."

There was a nod of assent, and Walker proceeded:

"I will not deny the fact that solicitude for Miss Hayward impels the act. But of this no more. Lieutenant Wells, you are unbound and unwatched. Place your sash across your breast, as worn by the officer of the day. I will give you the counter-sign, and thus you will be enabled to pass the pickets, and make good your escape. You can secure a safe retreat, and, after the excitement of the mur—of this unfortunate affair—has died away, Miss Hayward can be apprised of your place of concealment, and take such action in the case as her judgment or heart may dictate."

A deathlike silence reigned for a moment, during which rapid glances were exchanged between the friends. At length Wells asked:

"Captain Walker, would not an escape imply, upon my part, an acknowledgment of the crime of which I am accused?"

"It might, in the estimation of many. But, you are generally believed guilty. What matters it what your actions imply to *them*? Your friends here, who have already made up their minds, will merely look upon it as a desire upon your part to escape a certain, an unmerited, and a dishonorable death."

"And you will assist my flight?"

"I will."

"And will you afterward convey Miss Hayward to me if she will come?"

"With pleasure; you but anticipate my intended services."

Another rapid and significant glance passed between Mrs. Hinton and Wells, which was not observed by Walker.

"One thing more, Walker: do *you* believe me guilty of murder?"

"H'm—I *did*."

"And *now*?"

"I *may* have been mistaken. But, be that as it may, I will assist your flight."

"Are you ready?" asked Wells, rising.

"I wish you to return to your cell, and when all is ready, say *two or three o'clock*, I will come for you."

"But I will not go!" was the firm reply.

Walker perceived his mistake, and quickly added:

"As you please, sir." And turning, he was about to leave the tent, when he was confronted by the "officer of the day."

"Captain Walker," he said, sternly, "you feel an especial interest in Lieutenant Wells. I did not suppose so, but learned the fact from your conversation. I am glad you *do* feel so great a friendship for him. You shall have opportunity to make it manifest. You shall become his Pythias!"

"What do you mean, sir?"

"This: that the sentence of Lieutenant Wells will be read to-morrow afternoon at four o'clock. In the mean time, you, as his dear friend, do not wish to see him confined, and will most cheerfully take his place in the prison, and wear his chains. If the lieutenant is *present* to-morrow at four, you, as his hostage, will be released. If he should escape, as you have advised, of course you will be held as an aider and abettor in that escape; and when you receive that punishment your guilt deserves, you will have the consolation of knowing that you suffer for the benefit of your very dear friend! Soldiers," commanded the officer, "place the irons upon Captain Walker, and convey him to the guard-room in the old log-building."

"Are you mad? You *dare* not do it!" yelled Walker, as he foamed with rage. But the soldiers promptly obeyed the command, and Walker was taken from the tent.

"This indignity shall be avenged!" but he was carried quickly forward, and the guard-room door soon closed upon him.

"You will be at liberty, upon your parole of honor, until to-morrow at four o'clock, Lieutenant Wells."

The officers shook hands and separated.

CHAPTER VI.

The Gunpowder Plot and the Conspirator. The Mystery Unfolding.

JUST as the fading twilight was yielding to darkness, and before Lieutenant Wells had been removed from his cell by request of Alibamo, a scene occurred to which we must revert.

The room in which Wells was placed was in the wing of a log-house, just in the rear of the brick school-house to which we have alluded. Two doors led from this apartment, one opening into the garden, the other into the main building. This latter door had been firmly secured. Near that opening into the garden, was a small window, the only one in the apartment. As the guard was stationed at the door, escape from the room was impossible. Surrounding this garden were a number of hedges running in various directions, some of them forming the street fence, while others ornamented the winding gravel walks.

As soon as it was quite dark, a person closely enveloped and disguised, emerged from among the tents, and passed cautiously along in the still intenser darkness of the hedge shadow. Ever and anon he would pause and listen. Finally he reached the further hedge, remote from the camp. He paused a moment, and then gave a low and peculiar whistle. It was immediately answered, and two men joined the first comer.

"Are you ready?"

"No!" was the answer.

"And why not?"

"Because we have not received our pay."

"Is that the *only* reason?"

"The only reason after you have given us full instructions."

"Where is your powder?"

"In the upper part of the garden, under the hedge. We have secured eight twelve pound shells which we took from that battery over yonder. Powder enough to blow a mountain to the devil."

"Well, here is a hundred apiece. When the job is done, you will find as much more in the hollow log that I pointed out last night. Be careful and make sure work!"

"Well, your instructions!"

"You will follow the outer hedge. Creep along with great caution, and make no noise. There will be no danger, as the guard are not on the north side of the camp. When you reach the log-building in the rear of the brick school-house, you will observe a small wing, or addition, extending to the rear. At the back of this wing you will find an excavation under the house sufficiently large for your shells. Place them in it, lay your train, and then apply the torch. But you must do this with great caution, as a guard is stationed upon the opposite side."

"Don't be alarmed. Any one near that old log-shanty will go to kingdom come before to-morrow morning."

The trio then separated.

When Captain Walker was seized and chained by the soldiers, he made a desperate resistance, but in vain. He soon occupied the little room vacated by Lieutenant Wells. The door closed; he heard the clanking of the heavy chains which secured it, and left him in utter darkness. He stamped, and raved and cursed. Suddenly starting, and wildly clutching his throat, as if some terrible thought had crossed his mind, he groaned and sunk upon the floor.

"Fool! oh! fool that I was! I thought if I *pretended* friendship, and offered to assist in his escape, all suspicion of this night's work would be diverted from me. But now—oh! my God! What is the hour? Hark! I hear them working under the building! No! it is not the men yet. It is too early. I dare not tell the guard, for an acknowledgment of any suspicion of such a plot would be a confession of *my* guilt. Let me search for some mode of escape!"

Walker crawled cautiously around the floor, but not a crevice could be found. Finally, exhausted, he sunk down, giving way to his utter despair. An hour—two hours—dragged slowly by, which appeared an age of misery to the wretched man.

"If I give the alarm, even saying that a peculiar sound attracted my attention, the ruffians who are to do the work, will recognize me, and I shall, thus implicated, suffer an ignominious death! What is that? Great God! they are at work! But they are making so much noise that the guard will hear them, and I shall yet be saved!"

"Don't make quite so much noise in there, if you please!" exclaimed the guard, as he knocked upon the door where he was stationed.

"It is not me!" yelled the frantic man. "Some one is at the rear of the building, trying to dig through—they want to kill me!"

"We will see about that!" replied the guard, as he left his post, and walked toward the spot indicated.

Walker fell upon his knees and exclaimed:

"Oh! I am saved—saved that dreadful death!"

He bent down, and applying his ear to a small crevice between the logs, where the mud-mortar had fallen out, he listened. He could distinctly hear the words spoken.

"Have you silenced that d—d guard?" was asked.

"Yes, cut his wizzen. No danger. Hurry with the train of powder!"

"Gentlemen!" yelled Walker, "don't go any further. I am not the man!"

"Quick—fire the train!" exclaimed a voice outside.

A flash was seen, and then another said:

"Curse it, the train has failed. Throw the torch among the shells, and then run!"

Walker waited to hear no more, but throwing himself with all his violence against the door, he set up a series of yells, which made the camp ring. In a moment steps were heard, the door was thrown open, and Walker, livid with fear, and frantic, staggered into the open air, gasping for breath. When he had sufficiently recovered his fright to listen, the commander of the squad said:

"The powder-plot has been discovered, sir. There is no further danger on that head. But you will return to your cell!"

This order Walker was compelled to obey, and he was again left in darkness, with feelings better imagined than described.

The night wore slowly away. Lieutenant Wells had retired to his own tent. His calmness of demeanor certainly did not indicate a guilty mind. Alibamo, too, was wakeful, and strove by every possible kindness to sustain the heart and hopes of her suffering companion. Miss Nettie Morton, who had so recently joined their society, was occupying a tent in company with Miss Sally Long, near that of Mrs. Hinton. They also, were watchful—anxious for the morrow. But, perhaps, the most wretched person in that camp was Captain Hugh Walker. No officer would have dared to place irons upon him and confine him in a rough cell, upon any slight pretext. Was it not possible that something of a serious character had been discovered against him? This surmise seemed to haunt him, for he acted in a manner to indicate the wildest apprehensions of danger.

Morning came at last, and slowly the day advanced. A guard brought Walker his breakfast, but the man refused to answer any question. During the afternoon he heard the beating of the drums, and the bugle-blast, which he well understood was calling the division together for some important purpose. He felt satisfied that one object was the reading of the finding of the court-martial in the case of Lieutenant Wells. But, what part was *he* to play in the scene? This was the question which caused his heart to beat with violence, as the chains fell from the door of his prison, and he was called forth.

He accompanied the guard in silence, and soon entered the hollow square formed by the three brigades of the division. Walker glanced eagerly around, and there, standing beside the commanding General, was Lieutenant Wells, with Miss Hayward leaning upon his arm, and near them were their female friends. But a few paces distant were the two ruffians who had been engaged in the powder-plot. All was silent. The General advanced and said:

"Preliminary to other proceedings, I wish to ask Captain Walker if he ever before saw these two men?"

The ruffians advanced, rattling their chains. But Walker drew back, and with forced calmness he replied:

"I never have!" He dropped his head, gazing upon the ground.

The adjutant who held the sealed orders of the court-martial by which Lieutenant Wells had been tried, then advanced, and was about to commence reading the document in his hand, when a series of yells were heard, and in the distance was seen the grotesque form of Nettleton, as he came bounding along and bellowing:

"Stop the shootin'! Stop the shootin'!"

It was well known throughout the army that Nettleton had remained behind in search of Captain Hayward. As he approached, the most intense excitement was manifest. Lieutenant Wells could scarcely control his feelings, and would have rushed forward to meet Nettleton, had not Mrs. Hinton gently laid her hand upon his arm, begging him to be calm. Miss Hayward clung closer to her lover, as she hoped the news about to be brought by her brother's friend would relieve her agony of suspense. A half-suppressed cheer broke from the soldiers, as Nettleton burst into the square.

He paused for a moment, his breast heaving, and his eyes glaring wildly. But an instant was sufficient for him to discover that Wells was yet alive, and that the object of his suspicion also lived. He sprung forward, and, without uttering a word, seized Walker by the foot, which he at once drew under his arm; then he as suddenly bounded for the spot where the commandant was standing, dragging the foot along with him.

Of course this sudden movement on the part of Nettleton had thrown Walker violently upon his head, and, although he kicked, and squirmed and cursed, he was dragged along as if he had been a child.

When Nettleton reached the commander, he held the foot of Walker within a few inches of that officer's face, and yelled:

"Look! look! General—see them boots!"

Notwithstanding the intense anxiety felt for the result of Nettleton's search, the ridiculous figure he presented in his eagerness, and that of Walker who was twisting and struggling to escape, a general laugh ran through the division, which was joined in by the commander. Even Wells could not suppress a smile.

"And what about those boots?" asked the commander, after silence had been restored.

"Why, I've blacked them!" yelled Nettleton.

Another laugh was heard along the line.

"No doubt you have blacked them. But what of this?"

"Why, General, don't you see them *two hearts* made with nails, on the sole of that boot?"

"Certainly I see them. And what then?"

Walker was now permitted to resume his upright position, and he stood trembling with fear and rage, as Nettleton went on to relate his first suspicions of Walker, his search for the body of Captain Hayward, his finding the impression of the footprints standing side by side in the mud, at the edge of the stream, with the marks of *two hearts* in the sole of each boot; and then the finding of the handkerchief in the water, which Nettleton then produced.

The officer took the white linen witness, examining it closely, and then said:

"Here is the name of 'Walker,' in the corner. William, did you find this *near* the place where the murder was committed?"

"Right by the spot where them two boots stood!" replied Nettleton, pointing to Walker's feet.

"I can explain this," exclaimed Walker. "I went to the river that day to wash, and I stood upon the bank to do so. I presume I left the impression of my boots there at that time. If I did not, was I not also present in the morning to examine the spot where the murder had been committed? And is it a wonder that the impression of my boots should be left behind?"

"That is certainly true," replied the General. "But of the handkerchief?"

"It fell from my hands as I was washing, and I did not take the trouble to recover it."

"It is very probable!" replied the General.

"So you perceive," replied Walker, as he appeared to gain courage, "your trumped up evidence has fallen to the ground! I did not expect a combination of both officers and men against me, but I find it so. And they wish to see *me* suffer for the bloody deed done by that coward. The only reason I can assign for this persecution is, that he is in favor with the *ladies*, and you, sycophants that you are, hope, through him, to gain favor with his fair companions. No doubt some bargain to that effect already has been effected!"

Captain Walker had by this time become eloquent, and defiant. Nettleton, with his too eager perceptions, had failed to foresee the possible fallacy of his proofs, for hope and prejudice together had prevented any calm examination of his evidence. With a sorrowful and troubled look, he turned away. This gave Walker greater confidence, and, in a loud but hoarse voice he cried:

"And now I demand justice!"

"Which you shall have," replied the General. "But first answer me; how did this handkerchief, which bears your name, and which you confess to having used in the stream, become *bloody*?"

That was another point of interest, and Nettleton paused to listen attentively.

"I had a bleeding at the nose, and the reason I threw the dirty thing away, was, I did not think it worth washing!"

"Then some person must have recovered it, washed it very carefully, and thrown it into the stream again, for *there is* NO *blood upon it*!"

Walker attempted a reply, but his utterance failed. The General enjoined silence, and then stepping forward he said, in a voice sufficiently loud to be heard by all present:

"Captain Walker, I must sum up, before you, the evidence of crimes you have committed, which have no parallel in the history of the army, or of crimes which have ever been, or attempted to be committed in any civilized country. I would give you the benefit of a court-martial, were there any doubt of your guilt, and even *now* may *order* a trial, but it will only be a formal one. You had better confess your guilt, here, before all—ask their pardon—make reparation to those you have most injured, and die repentant!"

"I have nothing to confess!" responded Walker, bitterly.

"Have you no fear of the revelations of these two soldiers?" asked the General, pointing to the chained ruffians.

"I have no fear! No doubt they have been bribed to conspire with you! But, vent your spite! Go on!"

"Then, Captain Walker, I will briefly enumerate the circumstances which have been developed, as well as the *facts*. The morning we left Grand Prairie you were in command of the squad which escorted the prisoner, Lieutenant Edward Wells. You had not proceeded far when you were overtaken by two men. It was a very easy matter to secure an audience with you as you were in the rear of the division. They suggested that you should deliver Lieutenant Wells to them, as their commander had an especial spite against him, and wished to secure his person. You asked these men (I refer to the two ruffians now in chains and standing by your side,) how they dared to approach you on such a subject, and they replied that they had *witnessed your act* the evening previous, and that you need not put on airs with them! You then requested these fellows to meet you the next evening at the upper hedge. You instructed them to secure a number of pounds of powder for some purpose, which you would then explain. You met them the next evening. You gave them instructions. They were about to act upon them, when your outcries from the cell in which *you* had been placed, and which Lieutenant Wells had left only a short time previously, attracted the attention of the guard, and you were rescued. Prior to this you had offered to assist Lieutenant Wells to escape, but you wished him to return to his cell and remain until two or three o'clock. The fiendish act was to be committed between twelve and one. You *pretended* friendship, that all suspicion of the act might be diverted from you. Have I spoken correctly, sir?"

"No doubt you have spoken according to the story of those ruffians!" replied Walker. "You can not bring against me any *respectable* proof. I look to a court for the justice which I have no reason to expect here."

"Look!"

Walker, who had been shaking like a guilty wretch during the speech of the commander, turned in the direction indicated. The rough garb had fallen from the ruffians; their chains were thrown aside, and, to his astonishment and horror, there stood two of the regimental Union officers, ADJUTANT HINTON, the husband of Alibamo, and his friend, CAPTAIN CLARK!

Walker, who now saw how he had been entrapped, and detected in his infamy, for a moment was utterly unmanned. But, his resolute nature soon triumphed over his fear. Well realizing that penitence could not save him, he sprung to his feet and said:

"This is all a miserable, contemptible conspiracy—an effort to make out a case against me to shield that woman's pet from the consequences of his clearly proven crime. Hayward is dead, and can not be made to answer, else—"

"You lie, you dirty, nasty, murderin' skunk!"

"What!" exclaimed a dozen voices.

"He lies! the coward that stabs a man in the dark! Hayward is not dead, but lives, and will soon by his evidence send this murderer to kingdom come!"

With a shriek Miss Hayward bounded forward, and fell at the feet of Nettleton, grasping his hands. Wells, who had borne bravely up until this moment, covered his face, and wept tears of joy and of relief from the imputation of crime. Sally Long sprung to the side of Nettleton, and, throwing her arms around his neck she gave him a hearty kiss, which caused him to roll up his green eyes, and appear in almost as much agony as if he had been struck in the stomach with a cannon-ball. The word was soon passed, and the soldiers, catching the fire, made the very welkin ring with their shouts, while the band chimed in with the stirring strain: "Hail to the Chief!"

CHAPTER VII.

A Live Hero—The Retrograde Army Movement.

THE villain Walker was returned to his lonely cell. Lieutenant Wells was released from all restraint. The soldiers dispersed to talk about the strange turn events had taken, but the center of attraction was Nettleton. He was seated in front of the Hinton tent. Close beside him was Miss Hayward, kneeling, and gazing mournfully into his face, while Alibamo, Wells, the General, Nettie Morton, Sally Long, the officers who had composed the court-martial, the especial friends of the parties, and as many of the soldiers as could get within hearing distance, were earnestly listening to the narrative of the "body-guard."

Nettleton went on to relate his meeting the rebel scouts, and the fact of their having informed him that Hayward had only been wounded and conveyed toward Wilson's Creek, by a party attached to the command of Lieutenant-Colonel Price.

[The reader will mark the distinction between Lieutenant-Colonel Price, who was a ruffian guerrilla, and had broken his parole three times—an act repudiated by all honest soldiers of either army—and General Sterling Price, who, although a rebel, always had acted in a gentlemanly and humane manner to all prisoners of war.]

After listening to the story of William, the General drew from his pocket the note which had been found at the Ozark bridge, signed "Charles Campbell." This note must have been written but a few moments before the fight took place. The date would be just two days after Hayward had received the assassin's stroke, giving about the proper time for the wounded man to be carried from Grand Prairie to Ozark, at which latter place Lieutenant-Colonel Price had formed a temporary camp. The writer spoke of a wounded man in a boat, and against whom Price had an especial spite. This confirmed the conviction that Hayward had been taken thither for the especial gratification of Price's fiendish propensities. The note also said that he bore the marks of a captain's rank, and, in his delirium, spoke of "Net—" which might have referred to the young lady, Nettie Morton, whom he possibly might have seen in the distance, upon the bank, as the boat neared the spot where she was standing, or, as seemed more probable, that the wounded captain was calling upon Nettleton. At all events, it was decided that the person of whom Charles Campbell had written, was no other than Captain Hayward. It is true, he was still almost insensible from his wounds, and was near the camp of his most unforgiving enemy, but, there was a friend at hand—an enemy in arms—but a friend to the wounded and helpless soldier, as are all true men—and he had written that "he *would* save him!"

"Why should we not hope?" asked Alibamo, as she clasped her friend Mamie in her arms.

"And why should we not *act?*" cried Wells, as he clutched the hilt of his sword.

"Yes, we *will* act," yelled Nettleton, as he sprung up, and appeared ready for instant departure.

"Go, William; follow the stream from Ozark, until you find some trace, and then return to us," said Miss Hayward, eagerly.

Nettleton turned his gaze upon Miss Sally, for a moment, and then, as if ashamed of his hesitation, or of his weakness, in exhibiting *any* symptoms of love, he started with a bound, exclaiming:

"I'm off. Good-by, all!"

He had proceeded, however, but a few steps when he halted, and, scratching his head, his countenance assumed a most woful expression, and his eyes rolled wildly about.

"What is the matter, William?" asked Wells.

"*Got to go t'other way!*" was the melancholy reply.

"Why so?"

"O, just a bit of—fun—that's all!"

"Well, tell us what it is, Nettleton?"

"I can't! It will break *her* heart!" he replied, pointing to Sally.

"So it would, William, if any thing dreadful should happen to you!" replied Miss Long, as she dropped her eyes to the ground.

"There, didn't I tell you so?" replied the faithful servant, his mouth gaping and his eyes expanding.

"William," asked Wells, "do you really *love* Miss Long?"

"Love her, lieutenant? That ain't no name for it. Why, can't you see yourself that she's the sweetest darn sk— no, I mean the nicest critter in the world—exceptin' Miss Mamie!"

"And does she love you, William?" asked Alibamo, smiling in spite of herself at the tableau enacting before her.

"*Of course I do!*" replied Sally, proudly and triumphantly, as if a victory had been won.

"There—there! Do you hear that? Now, don't you pity me? I believe I am the most ugly cuss in the world. I never thought anybody would ever love *me*, and now I find out the gal as I wants most is just the one as does love me! Oh Lordy, I'm sick, I do believe!"

"All right!" Wells responded, with a smile.

"All right! Not by a blasted sight, sir! Did *you* think it all right when you loved Miss Mamie, and thought you had to swing?"

"What! You talk in riddles. Explain."

"*I've got to be hung!*" he roared, but, whether with pain or delight, none could tell.

"Why, *you* didn't have any thing to do with hurting the captain?" cried Sally, as she advanced toward her beloved.

Nettleton gazed at her an instant with a most singular expression, and then replied:

"Miss Long, never let suspicion cross that delicate bo— mind of yours, but like the true turtle-dove, put your trust in the uprighteousness of your future lord and master, what is to be hanged all on account of the first time you wrapped them delicate arms of yourn around my long neck."

"William, what do you mean by being hanged?" asked the General.

Nettleton then went on to relate the agreement he had made with Price, to return, and undergo the punishment which was about to be inflicted upon him when that General interfered. He declared his intention of returning at once, as his "furlough" had run out, and as a "man of honor" he must return.

"And do you really intend to return?" asked the General.

"*Of course I do!*" replied William, with something of scorn and much of pride in his tones.

"William, think for a moment. You are now safe. You are with one who loves you, and with whom you can be happy. Why will you return?"

"General, don't argue this point with me. I said I would come back, and darn me if I don't!" Nettleton started, after having shook the hand of his friends.

"Stay a moment, Nettleton," said the General. "I have a letter from General Price with regard to you."

Nettleton paused and listened, as the commander, opening the envelope, read:

"Camp near Cassville, Nov. 12th, 1861.

"*To General* ——, *greeting*.

"A prisoner of war was released from our camp, and permitted to return to Springfield, on the 9th. It was at first thought that he was a spy, as he had been seen in and near our camp before, and he was about to suffer death upon the scaffold, when I saw and questioned him. I became convinced that he was no spy, but a faithful servant and friend, searching for his captain, whom he loved. I ordered his release. I gave him a parole of honor. He promised to return that the sentence of the 'drum-head court' could be carried into effect upon him, after he had given the evidence he possessed, which he declared was necessary to save an innocent man. I admire his truthfulness. Should he be determined to return, of which I have no doubt, you will read this letter, which releases William Nettleton from any further obligation. He will remain with his friends, and be happy.

"Signed by the A. A. A. G.

"For the Commander, PRICE."

The effect upon the gallant fellow of the reading of this letter, was somewhat singular. He stood for a moment gaping around upon the spectators, as if he had been caught in some mean act. Then a smile came over his face like sunlight creeping over a rugged mountain top. Soon his countenance looked like a newly risen sun—fairly blazing with blushes. Then, with a wild *whoop*, which rung out like a signal, he sprung into air, rattled his feet together, and once on earth again, bounded off like a great moose, for the nearest thicket, where to indulge his "feelings" without restraint.

The crowd dispersed in good-humor, to talk over the strange events of an hour. If one heart was happier than all, it was that of poor Mamie, whose joy at the proven innocence of her friend and lover was too intense for words. In her heart a new hope had also arisen, that her dear brother would again be restored to her arms, and thus fill up the cup of her blessings to the brim.

It had been decided by the friends of Hayward, that a search for the captain would be useless, but it was hoped that Charles Campbell would give some information which would lead to his discovery, or that Fall-leaf, a celebrated Indian scout, who had now been absent many days on the very line of the enemy's march, would return with some tidings, by which the actions of the captain's anxious friends should be governed.

The Army of the Mississippi, having passed from Fremont's command to that of General Hunter, had been ordered to fall back from Springfield, in two columns. The one by the way of the Osage and Warsaw to Tipton, Mo., on the line of the main Pacific road, and the other by way of Lebanon, on the main road between Springfield and Rolla, the south-western branch of the same road. Each place, in distance from Springfield, was about one hundred and twenty-five miles.

The march of the division to which Captain Hayward's friends were attached, which was under the command of the brave Sigel, was commenced on the morning of November 20th. That division formed the rear of the entire army. It proceeded by the Rolla turnpike.

Nothing of note transpired until the division was ascending the rolling hill about two miles before reaching Lebanon, when a horseman, his face and head streaming with blood, rode rapidly along the lines, exclaiming:

"Fight in front! Fight in front!"

He halted for no one to question him, but kept on his way. No guns were heard, and many expressed the opinion that it must be a strange fight. But, as a necessary precaution, the infantry-men were halted, their pieces loaded, and bayonets fixed. The artillery was charged, and flags unfurled. As the troops ascended the hill, and looked in vain for a foe, the question was asked: "Where is the fight?"

This was soon settled, as another messenger rode up and informed the General that a party or squadron of rebel cavalry, numbering about four hundred, had attacked a little band of "home guards," of about thirty, which had been collected in a valley some twenty miles south of Lebanon, on the main road, in a place called "Bohannan Mills valley." Most of the thirty "home guard" had been killed, wounded or dispersed by the guerrillas. Then all families in that vicinity known to entertain Union proclivities, were visited at the dead of night. "Murder and arson" was the cry. Many poor creatures soon were in the agonies of death. Husbands, who had rushed from concealment to defend their wives, had been cloven to the earth; children ran shrieking to and fro, only to be dashed to pieces by the savages of the Missouri Mountain. It was a carnival of lust and blood, over which the historian ever must dwell in horror. And yet, these fiends in human shape were protected by the ægis of the "Confederate" flag!

Such was the scene depicted by the messenger, when the division was halted, and a consultation took place. It was decided that, while the main army went forward, two companies of infantry, a section of artillery, and a company of cavalry, should be detached to proceed at once to "Bohannan Mills," to protect the helpless families, and, if possible, to punish the rebel horde which had committed such awful crimes against humanity.

CHAPTER VIII.

Gone!—The Signal Song.

WE must now take the reader back to Springfield. It was one week after the exposure and confinement of Walker, and something like a month before the army had commenced its retrograde movement, as described in the foregoing chapter.

Walker, after the first paroxysm of his rage was over, settled himself down to think. Although he had shown a bold front at first, his final conviction drove from his heart all resolution, and he evinced the most abject cowardice—the cowardice of conscious guilt, which makes the strongest tremble.

But Walker was not a man to sit quietly in his cell, and submit to his fate. His mind having been settled in the conviction that certain death would follow, he began to form his plans of action. To arrive at any definite conclusion was no easy matter, as he was chained, and a double guard placed around his quarters. Yet he had hope—time was given and all might yet be right. He learned that he was not to be tried by a division court-martial, but would be removed to St. Louis, in order that a general court might act upon his case. He also learned that it would be at least a month, before the army would take up its march. Thus he had time—time precious to him—for, like all shrewd villains, he had his confederates, even in the army as well as out of it, and to these he now looked for his bodily safety.

It was the third night of his incarceration, that, springing to his feet, he listened intently. There were three distinct taps on the door.

"The rescuers—the gang—I'm saved!" he muttered, as he gave three taps on the door, in response.

"What's the word?" was asked from the outside.

"C. S. A. and the Bars!" answered Walker. "And you?"

"Good! Union against oppression!"

"To-night?" asked Walker, with eagerness.

"No, the pal on the other side ain't for Union. Can't before day after to-morrow. Jim goes on then, and though it ain't my turn, I think I can get pony No. 2 drunk, and the job can be done. I'll try."

"Be cautious. Trust no one without the word. It was the neglect on my part, thinking it all right, to demand the 'words,' which brought me into this scrape!"

The "rounds" approached, and the sentinel was relieved.

Nothing of importance transpired in camp for the next three days. An unusual quiet prevailed. It is true, there was much talk upon the subject of the attempted murder, and many expressions of bitterness against Walker. Some even went so far as to suggest the hanging of that wretch before the army left Springfield, lest he should escape. None were more vehement than a repulsive looking soldier, known throughout camp as "ugly Jim!" He stated that he had been on guard only a few nights before in front of the prisoner's quarters, and that he had every reason to believe Walker was trying to escape, adding that he wished he had been satisfied of the fact, as he would have been glad of an opportunity to put a bullet through the murderous scoundrel.

The party had been drinking freely, and had become exceedingly communicative. One of the soldiers, whose post was No. 1 on guard duty that night—that is, in front of the prisoner's door—swore he would shoot Walker if he could find any pretext.

"*You* have no spite against him," exclaimed ugly Jim, "and *I* have. Let *me* take the matter in hand. I will stand your guard, and if the villain attempts to move, I'll riddle him, sure as Potosi lead mines."

"Enough said. I am on the second relief. I go on at seven and off at nine; again at twelve and off at two. This will be your time."

"Good! I shall be on hand!"

Ugly Jim then approached the tent of Miss Hayward, and requested an audience alone with that lady. It so happened that she was alone, Alibamo having gone to visit her husband, and Sally being at the time strolling through the camp with Nettleton.

"If you wish to learn all the particulars about your brother, I think you can do so," said Jim, in a tone of great kindness.

"Oh! in what manner?" asked Miss Hayward, eagerly.

"I don't exactly know. But I will tell you what I *do* know. You see I am on guard to-night from twelve till two, over the cell of Walker. I don't like the villain any way, but, he told me if I would get you to come to him, he would tell you all he knows of the matter!"

"Certainly I will go. Call Alibamo, and we will go together, at once!"

"I will," answered Jim, as he turned to depart. Then pausing, he added:

"Miss Hayward, now I recollect that Walker said you must come alone. He declared he would not commit himself by speaking before any one."

"I dare not go alone!"

"Poor child!" exclaimed Jim, as he wiped his eyes. "Do you think you *can* be alone when this old soldier, as folks call 'ugly Jim,' is near you? I know my face is ugly, but I don't think my heart is! Besides, you won't *see* the wretch himself. You will only talk to him through a crack between the logs, and I shall be as close to you as Walker will allow. Of course he wont let *me* hear what he says, but I shan't let you be out of my sight, so there will be no danger!"

"Why can we not go at once?" asked Miss Hayward.

"Because I don't go on post until twelve o'clock, and the other guard wouldn't let you speak to him."

"Then I will come at quarter past twelve. But I shall rely upon you for protection!"

"You may do that, miss. And I really think you do right. I know Walker is a *very* bad man, but he has got to die, and may be he wants to make a confession to relieve his mind, and to ask your pardon. And I always think it best to give a dying man a chance to relieve his mind, and confess."

"You may expect me!"

Jim bowed, and left the tent.

Twelve o'clock came; the guard was relieved, and "ugly Jim" had taken the place of his *sick friend*, in front of Walker's prison. All was quiet, save the clanking of a chain, a few hurried whispers, and the opening and closing of a heavy door, which sounds were in close proximity to Walker's dungeon. The words "*C. S. A. and Bars*" were answered by "*Union against Oppression,*" and two dark forms glided to concealment beside the thorn hedge, while the guard remained at the door.

The evening dragged slowly along for Miss Hayward. A hundred times she had almost resolved to communicate to her friends the fact of her intended visit to Walker, and to ask their advice, and, if need be, to request that some one should follow in the distance, to lend assistance, should any be required. But what had she to fear? Walker was secure in his cell, and one of the faithful guard had promised his protection. Besides, she had promised to go alone. If she did not, it would imply suspicion of an honest soldier. Walker might also ask if she had come entirely unattended, and how could she answer him?

Miss Hayward was naturally timid, and by no means self-reliant. When the news of the supposed death of her brother reached her, she was almost paralyzed with grief. But, now that hope had filled her heart, she began to nerve herself to the task of unremitting search, even though she must encounter the greatest dangers.

The hour of twelve arrived. Closely muffled in a cloak, she crept from her tent, and then paused to listen. She heard nothing, save the slow and regular breathing of the sleepers, and the violent beating of her own heart. She started, but her steps seemed to fail her, and she leaned against a tree for support. The thought of her dear brother, and the probable unraveling of the mystery which surrounded his attempted assassination, and his present fate, gave her renewed courage, and she sped onward. In a few moments she had cleared the camp, and arrived in the center of the garden, where stood the doomed man's prison. As she neared the door, the guard asked:

"Is that you, Miss Hayward?"

"It is!" came the low response.

"Approach and fear nothing."

She had barely reached the threshold, when two forms, darting from beneath the hedge, threw a heavy blanket over her head, thus entirely smothering any attempt, on her part, to give the alarm. Who and what her captors were, she could not divine, or what might be their purpose. Strange to say, her reason did not forsake her. She felt herself borne rapidly along, but not a word was spoken. It appeared to her that hours passed by, and she even longed to hear some word uttered which might give a clue to the intentions of those in whose power she was, or to throw some light upon the subject, as to whom her captors were. The blanket, which was very heavy, almost causing suffocation, had been removed, and a lighter one substituted.

At length the parties halted, and, seating themselves upon the ground, the covering was removed, and Miss Hayward was permitted to gaze around her. Her eyes first met those of Captain Walker. She shuddered, and turned away. Then glancing at his two companions, she at once recognized "ugly Jim," and a person known in camp as "stupid Dick," both of whom had served as Union soldiers, for a long time, under Walker. As her eyes met those of "ugly Jim," she exclaimed:

"Oh! *you* will protect me?"

A laugh was the only reply.

"I trust Miss Hayward will permit *me* to become her protector!" said Walker, in an assumed tone of kindness.

Miss Hayward did not reply, but gazed around her. She was in a wild spot. She was seated beside a lovely stream of water, in a deep valley, while high on either hand were ragged hills or mountains. She knew the country for at least ten or twelve miles from Springfield in all directions was quite level, and she judged she must be near the Ozark country, the first range of whose ridges she had frequently seen from that point.

"Does not the lovely Miss Hayward deign a reply to her most devoted lover?" asked Walker.

"What was your purpose in tearing me from my friends, and conveying me here?" asked Miss Hayward.

"A pardonable one, I think. My life was forfeited in the Federal camp, and personal interest required me to depart. I could not think of leaving without you, and so I resorted to a little stratagem. My love for you must plead my excuse."

"But I have told you, Captain Walker, that I could not love you. Do you suppose after what has transpired that I could entertain any other feeling toward you than detestation?"

"I am aware of that. But, when you know me better, I am sure you will consent to reward my devotion. I am going to convey you to your brother!"

"Then I *will* thank you, at least!" exclaimed Miss Hayward.

"Nothing else?"

She shuddered.

"I must be plain with you," continued Walker. "I am *not* what I have seemed to be while with the Federals. I am a colonel in the Confederate army, but I accepted a commission in the so-called Union army, that I might furnish information to my Generals. Or, if you like the term better, you may call me a spy. These two soldiers have been with me for the same purpose. And we were not alone. There are now, in the army of the Mississippi, over three hundred privates, and over twenty officers, who *pretend* loyalty to the Federal cause; and I think, when his sister has become the wife of Captain Walker, or Colonel Brown, he may be induced to join us!"

"Will you take me to my brother?"

"On one condition, I will."

"And this condition?"

"Miss Hayward, I love you with all the ardor of my soul. You have become necessary to my very existence—*are* a part of my life. When you spurned me, it drove me frantic, and I am so now. Beware—oh! beware how you turn this heart, which is yet pure, so far as you are concerned, into a hell of furies! Pity me! Oh! dear Miss Hayward, pity me!"

"But my brother—what of him?"

"I will tell you of your brother when you have answered my questions."

"Proceed, sir!"

"Do not speak so coldly. I will be frank with you. Your brother is a prisoner—not in the Confederate camp, but in a secure place, on the very stream beside which you are now sitting. The murmuring and singing of these very waters will, ere two hours, greet his ears with the same strain. Warble those strains to which I have so often listened while in camp, and which stirred my soul, and they will be borne direct to your brother's hearing, to relieve his brain perhaps from the insanity which now enchains him!"

"Insanity!" echoed Mamie. "My brother insane?"

"He is a raving maniac! And but one thing can restore him!"

"Oh wretched, horrible news! What *can* I do to save my brother?"

"You are the only person who *can* save him. Nor is the task a hard one. Only a few miles from here is a Confederate camp. A chaplain is in attendance. He will perform the ceremony which will make you irrevocably and securely mine. Go with me. Become my wife, and to-morrow I will take you to your brother, and we will not only restore his shackled feet to liberty, but his shattered senses to reason. We alone can do it. Can you assume the responsibility of a refusal?"

Miss Hayward remained silent for a few moments, and then gazed alternately at the three villains. An unnatural fire lit up her eyes. At length she said:

"Captain Walker, I do not know but you are even now deceiving me. You may not know any thing about where my brother is."

"Ask these soldiers," replied Walker.

Miss Hayward turned her eyes upon them.

"The captain speaks right," answered Jim. "He *does* know where your brother is. He *is* crazy and is chained in the—"

"Silence!" commanded Walker. "Do you believe, Miss Mamie?"

"I must believe the worst," answered Miss Hayward. "Soldiers," she added, turning to the soldiers, "do you believe in the truth of Captain Walker's profession of love for me?"

"I should like to know why not!" replied Jim, doggedly. "Nobody could *help* loving you; even I loves you, but I know it ain't no use, and so I don't say nothing!"

"What have *you* to say?" asked Mamie, turning to the other soldier.

"Lord, Miss Mamie, I allers loved you, but 'stupid Dick' never thinks of such as you, and so I acted mean just to spite!"

"Gentlemen," cried Miss Hayward, springing to her feet, "listen to me. You have wronged me deeply, by aiding this wretched villain, your captain, to abduct me. I despise, loathe him; and, sooner than become *his* wife, I would permit my brother to die as he is, for I know that he would curse me were I to save him at such a sacrifice. It will be *but* death, and I shall suffer very little, for my brother's pure soul will scarce have taken its flight, ere mine will follow!"

"Miss Hayward!"

"Silence, Captain Walker. Soldiers, you have human hearts, and this man has not. I appeal to you. Save me! Find my brother and return him safely, and I promise to pay you one thousand dollars each. If I fail to do this, I swear, by the hope of heaven, that I will become the wife of one of you, the choice to be decided by lots between you!"

These words acted like an electric shock upon the soldiers. They sprung to their feet and confronted Walker. But he had anticipated the effects of her words, and stood sword and revolver in hand.

"You would play me false!" demanded Walker, fiercely.

"Guess I would!" replied Jim.

"Take that, then!" yelled Walker.

The report of a pistol echoed through the valley, and Jim fell without so much as a groan.

"And how do *you* decide?" asked Walker, turning and pointing his revolver toward Dick.

"I was only goin' to help you. I ain't no such foolish cuss as to think of marrying a fine lady like that! I'm all right!"

"Prove yourself so, and you shall *have* your thousand. Deceive me, and you share his fate!"

As Walker spoke he stepped to a clump of thick bushes, and drew a small boat from concealment. Handing Miss Hayward to a seat, and preceded by Dick, Walker entered, and the little craft swept gently along with the current, down the stream.

They had proceeded but a short distance, when Miss Hayward burst forth, and sung a wild, thrilling air, which echoed far and wide, through the valley and across the hills. There was something strangely beautiful in her song, and something still more strange in her actions. As each strain echoed over the hills, and gave back the ringing notes, she would start, and listen attentively, and a gleam of joy would lighten up her pale face, upon which a shade of disappointment would almost as soon appear. Her hearers sat in silence, and in apparent wonder.

"Those words are significant!" exclaimed Walker. "What is their import?"

"*She's* going mad, too, I opine!" exclaimed Dick. "Better *let* her go!"

"Silence!" cried Walker. "Miss Hayward, do you think your voice will penetrate *his* retreat?"

She made no answer, but, as the little boat swept onward, ever and anon the same words, and the same wild music broke the stillness of the forest, now sounding like a wail of sorrow, and then becoming almost hushed in hopeful expectation. The words had the appearance of being extemporized for the occasion, and were as follows:

Break those fetters—I am calling—

Listen *only* to my song!

I am waiting—loved one—waiting!

I have waited—oh, so long!

Give but one fond word to cheer me,

As I pray, and hope, and weep!

Let *thy echo* say thou'rt near me,

As my vigils thus I keep!

Echo, as along I glide,

This my song, from thy retreat,

And I'll bound to thy dear side!

Are we e'er again to meet?

Yes, a Seraph from on high

Whispers to me, thou art nigh!
Friends are waiting—friends are near—
Dearest brother—do not fear!

CHAPTER IX.

The Pursuit—The Perilous Situation—Important Information.

It was two o'clock in the morning, nearly two hours after Miss Hayward had been seized, and borne from the camp by Walker and his confederates. The guard relief had commenced his rounds. The first post visited was that in front of the door where Walker had been confined. A glance revealed the prisoner's escape. The chain which had secured the door was lying upon the steps, and the door itself was slightly ajar. Walker and both the sentinels had disappeared. The "long roll" was at once beaten, and the camp aroused. Scarce had the lines been formed when it was announced that Miss Hayward also had disappeared. The grief of her friends, and the rage of the soldiers knew no bounds, and many was the oath of a terrible retribution uttered against the fiend who had spread such desolation and sorrow in her path.

It was but a few moments before squads of cavalry were dashing in every direction in pursuit. There was but little doubt as to how the escape had been effected. The disappearance of the guard convinced all that they were in league with Walker, but in what manner they had gained possession of Miss Hayward was a mystery. No one had detected any thing unusual in her manner the evening before, and she had retired at her usual hour.

It was thought, however, that the parties would not have taken any main road, as the pickets would have given the alarm. They could not have had more than two hours the start, as every thing was all right when the twelve o'clock relief went on post, and at two o'clock the escape was discovered. If Walker had to walk through the fields in order to avoid the pickets, it would take at least two hours to clear them. It was most likely that, once outside the lines, friends and horses would be procured. Still, the distance would not be so great but that our horsemen hoped to overtake them, and so they set off with a good will in various directions.

"Are *you* not going to accompany us?" asked Lieutenant Wells, of Nettleton, who was seated upon the ground, looking gloomy and sullen.

"Not by a darn sight!" answered Nettleton, doggedly.

"And why not?" asked Wells.

"You go 'long, and let me alone!" he answered, sharply.

There was no time for words, and the squadron departed.

The night passed, during which Nettleton was bitter in his self-reproach for not watching closer, and would not hold conversation with any person. As the first dawn of day became visible, Nettleton was seen crawling upon his hands and knees, in front of the former prison of Walker, and through the garden, toward the west. His movements were watched with considerable interest, as all had begun to respect him for his sagacity, in his peculiar way. At length he returned to his tent, and, without speaking, carefully examined his double-barrel shot gun—a beautiful piece which he had picked up upon the Wilson creek battle-ground, and had been permitted to retain. This he loaded; then, taking a large artillery ammunition-bag, he went directly to the tent of Adjutant Hinton. Removing the lid of a minnié-ball ammunition-box, he filled this pouch with cartridges. His next move was to place some provision in his haversack; then he started.

"Where are you going, William?" asked Mrs. Hinton.

"Them *boots*!" he replied, pointing in the direction he had just taken in his hands-and-knees examination.

"What do you mean?"

"Why, *them boots as had two hearts on the soles* went *that* way, and I'm going to follow if I go to thunder!" He waited to hear no more, or to speak more, but bounded off to the westward.

He had been gone perhaps an hour, when Fall-leaf, the Indian scout already referred to, entered the camp. He was soon made aware of the state of things. Fall-leaf was deeply attached to Captain Hayward, and, more especially so to his fair sister, Mamie. The scout had been but a short time in camp, when he had given to the General all the information he possessed with regard to the enemy. This done, he followed on the trail fast as possible.

For several hours Nettleton kept on his course, now striking the main road for the purpose of searching for fresh tracks, then taking to the woods again, to avoid observation. Several times he came upon the well-known footprints, and a bitter exclamation would escape him. He kept his course, more from the judgment he had formed as to the direction Walker had taken, than from the numerous impressions of his boots. He was ascending a sharp and ragged hill, so heavily covered with the thorn-bush and small scrub-oak peculiar to that country, that his progress was rendered very difficult. Suddenly a figure darted in front of him and concealed itself among the thick undergrowth. Nettleton brought his gun to the shoulder, and called out:

"None of that skulking, darn ye! Come out and fight fair!"

"Ugh!" responded the voice, and Fall-leaf bounded to his side.

"Oh! it's you, is it, Mr. Ingen? Well, I'm darn glad you've come, for you can hunt these snarly woods better than me! Any news?"

"You kill 'em—eh?"

"I shall kill 'em, if I only get a bead on the critter!"

"You *did* kill 'em?"

"Kill who?"

"Dead soldier—there!" Fall-leaf indicated that he meant further on.

"Come on, Ingen," said Nettleton. He reached the summit of the hill which overlooked the valley below, and, led by Fall-leaf, began its descent. They soon reached the stream, and the Indian pointed to the dead body. Nettleton gazed upon it a moment, and then said:

"Darn me if it ain't the very feller what run away last night. Walker has been here, sure!"

He commenced his search at once. He found footprints in the sand, and among them that of a lady, judging from its small size. The Indian had also been taking observations. Returning from a clump of bushes, he said to Nettleton:

"See—canoe—two—White Bird—so!"

Here Fall-leaf indicated by action, that two men had drawn a boat from concealment in the thicket, had entered it, as indicated by tracks in the sand, and had proceeded down-stream.

"Well, they've got rid of one scoundrel, any way. It will only be man to man, and I feel myself to be a match for any dozen such skunks as that Walker. They can't have much the start!"

Both Fall-leaf and Nettleton walked rapidly forward along the bank of the stream. At length—and it was almost a simultaneous movement on the part of each—they stopped, and bending forward, held their ears close to the ground.

"By thunder!" cried Nettleton, "that's *her* voice!"

"White Bird caged—*she* no sing!" replied Fall-leaf.

"Ain't you a darn fool? Don't you know that White Bird, as you call her, has got a right to expect some of her friends will be after her, and so she sings that they may hear her voice, echoing up and down among these hills, and know where to find her?"

"Ugh! good—white hunter no fool!"

Again the voice was heard, and this time so clearly as to leave no doubt upon the mind of our hero, as to who the singer was. Like a deer he bounded off in the direction indicated. The music died away and all was still. But the two men paused not.

Upon a sudden they emerged into an open field of about four acres, near the center of which were two large stacks of hay. The river at this point took a bend, and the two pursuers struck directly across the open space. Just as they reached the stacks, Fall-leaf darted close in to the base of one of them, taking the attitude of a listener, and making a significant sign to Nettleton.

"What is it?" asked Nettleton.

"Hark! Soldiers! Horses! Whoa! Hark!"

Nettleton listened attentively, and then said:

"There is a party of soldiers coming. It *may* be our men who have been in search of Miss—— of the White Bird; but, it is well enough to keep close. It may be the rebels merely moving camp. And if this is so, Mamie must be with them. The sounds are coming nearer—crawl under the hay, red-skin—way under, out of sight."

This was effected with some difficulty, when a party of rebel guerrillas, numbering about sixty, rode into the field, and proceeded to form their camp directly in the vicinity of the hay-stacks, under which the two men were concealed.

"Well, I guess we've got into the right shop!" said Nettleton to Fall-leaf. "We are cooped up here close enough for a while, but, Miss Mamie must be with this crowd, and when dark comes, we can scout around and see what we can do. Lay quiet, Ingen!"

"White hunter knows! Make good Ingen!"

The day dragged slowly away. Toward night a party of the rebels came for forage for their horses, but the hay was tumbled from the top of the stack, and our friends were not discovered. The guerrillas' conversation, however, was listened to with the greatest interest by Nettleton.

"So Colonel Brown, or Walker, as he is called, came within one of being done for in the camp of the Yanks at Springfield?"

"Yes, so he says."

"What the devil does he want with the gal?"

"Oh, some love affair, of course."

"The gal was happy, for she was singing like a nightingale."

"Oh yes! No doubt she was dazzled by the prospect of being a colonel's wife."

"Who is she?"

"Don't know."

"My eyes! but she *is* a beauty!"

"So much the better for him."

"Where was he going with her?"

"Oh, below—taking her to her brother, I believe."

"Where is that?"

"Down in the *old mill.*"

This was all the conversation heard by the adventurers. But, the rebel troops did not move again until late in the next day, and our friends were compelled to remain quiet. They had learned sufficient to convince them that Miss Hayward was *not* with this band of rebels, but was being borne still further from them. They cursed the chance which had thus entrapped them, and prevented their overtaking the captive at once. Still, they resolved to keep up the pursuit, and they had learned that at *some mill* the lady was to be conveyed, and that her brother was there. Patiently they waited until they could emerge, and finish their journey.

CHAPTER X.

Hayward.

IT is time the reader was enlightened, somewhat, as to the fate of Captain Hayward.

The wound he had received the night of the attempted assassination, was severe, but by no means fatal. The loss of blood had rendered him very weak, and for some time he remained insensible.

At the moment the blow was inflicted, there was, upon the other bank of the river, and watching the Federals, a squad of rebel cavalry scouts. The water into which Hayward was thrown soon revived the wounded man. He was seen by this band, and carried to the house of an officer of the Confederate army, not half a mile from the spot. Here his wound was dressed. It was not long before an order reached them, signed by "Colonel Brown," to convey him to the camp of Colonel Price, at Ozark. This order was law, and immediately after the Federals left Grand Prairie, a boat was procured, and Hayward placed in it. But half conscious, he reached the Ozark bridge at the critical juncture already described in the chapter referring to the interview between Nettie Morton and Charles Campbell, and the interruption by Colonel Price, the rescue of Nettie by Fall-leaf, the approach of the Union forces, and the resolve of Charles Campbell to save the wounded captain.

It was at the moment when Price was in pursuit of the Indian that Campbell, taking advantage of his absence, and observing the approach of the Federals, hastily penned the note previously referred to and then pushed off with the boat, down the stream, in order to effect his escape with the prisoner.

He began to hope that success would crown his efforts. The battle favored his flight. All that day and the night following, he pursued his course. It was his purpose to follow the Gasconade until he had reached the point nearest Rolla, where he supposed he would be free from the roving bands of rebels, who were so numerous in the vicinity of Springfield. But his hopes were doomed to disappointment. Colonel Price, anticipating the direction he had taken, immediately dispatched one Lieutenant Lewis, a most tireless wretch, with a squad of ten men, to intercept Campbell, and the prisoner captain.

Just as the morning dawned, Campbell saw the pursuing party approaching. Pulling for the shore, he lifted Captain Hayward in his arms, and bore him into a mill, which stood near at hand. There he quickly concealed his charge in an upper loft, and returned to meet the rebels. He stated he had been captured by a party of the Federals and conveyed to that point, and that they had there released him upon his parole of honor. This story was generally believed, although one of the band appeared to be incredulous, and left his fellows for a pretended search. Not observing his absence, the remainder of the rebel band returned without him, taking care, however, that Campbell was not left behind.

When this person entered the mill, he found Hayward leaning upon his elbow, quite conscious, but too weak to move. He paused before the wounded man, and was silent, Hayward saw, and recognized him.

"Are friends near?" was his feeble question.

"I am the only friend you have got in these parts, and I reckon as how 'ugly Jim' ain't just the man you want to see!"

"You are one of my own men!" returned Hayward.

"That's a p'int as will admit of some argument, as the lawyers say! I may be *your* man when I am in Springfield, but you are *my* man now! So don't kick up any fuss, and after I have made you fast, I'll tell you the rest. Ha, ha!" he muttered to himself, "but Walker shall pay me well for *this*!"

Saying this the rebel rascal left the mill. Not far from this mill, in a wretched log-hut, lived an old woman, who gloried in the title of "crazy Madge," and of whom the rude backwoods people of the vicinity stood in fear, as it was almost universally believed among them that she was possessed of the devil. She told fortunes with great correctness, and employed the most singular modes in doing this, such as burning powder and strange incense, and the uttering of fearful imprecations, and unearthly sounds.

The mill was owned by one Bohannan, a captain of Confederate guerrillas. Since the commencement of the war, it had not been in operation, except on rare occasions. About one mile above Bohannan's mill, there was another mill, of smaller dimensions, which had formerly been owned by a thorough Union man, who, becoming a refugee, had abandoned this mill, also. So when the residents in that region, or any of the straggling rebel bands, had occasion to grind their grain, they always went to the upper mill, more especially as it was believed that "crazy Madge" had taken full possession of the lower one after its proprietor left, and that, being occupied in sacrilegious rites, it was very generally believed to be unsafe to venture in that vicinity. Even the most reckless and hardy of the guerrillas held the spot in awe, and avoided it at all times.

Madge was seated in her own door when Campbell entered the mill with Hayward in his arms. She watched him closely, but uttered no word. She saw him emerge, and meet the rebel band. She watched their departure, and then discovered the newcomer, "Grouse Green," as he was known. When he came forth from the mill, Madge still was seated in the cabin doorway, smoking her pipe. She did not even raise her eyes, or pretend the least consciousness of his presence, until, with a rude slap upon her shoulder, he said:

"Come, old woman, I want you!"

The old creature pretended not the least surprise, but, raising her snake-like eyes to those of the speaker, she said:

"Does the son of Belial wish to know his fate? I need not the aid of my magic charms to point it out to me. In less than a month, the most horrible death—"

"Bah, you old crone! I'd dash your brains out for a copper, you infernal croaking old buzzard! I don't come to have my fortune told, but I want you to serve me, and you shall have gold—do you hear, old woman? No fooling now, and gold is yours!"

"Gold! It is the master-key to human hearts! And what am I to do for gold?"

"My bidding! First, I want a set of chains! Have you such things in your infernal den?"

"You can have them for gold!" she exclaimed, tottering to a closet, and rattling the cold iron. "I always keep them—it is necessary to my trade!"

"Now for the bargain, old hag. You saw me enter that mill just now? Well, there is a captain confined, or will be confined before I leave him, in the upper loft. He will be fastened. You must feed him daily, just enough to keep life in him. I will give you a hundred to start upon—more money than you ever saw, old woman, and when I return, if you have well done your duty as keeper, I will give you another hundred. Will you be faithful and keep the prisoner in safety from rescue?"

"I swear it by my magic art!"

"Bah! blast your art! Swear it by the gold you will receive, and I'll believe you. But come!"

Green reëntered the mill followed by old Madge. He seized the helpless Hayward and bore him to an upper loft. There he fettered him with the chains.

"And now I shall leave you here until we can attend to you at a more convenient time!" he muttered, as he gazed exultingly upon Hayward. He was about to leave him alone.

"Stay but a moment!" cried the wounded man. "Tell me of my sister!"

"She has become the wife of Colonel Brown, of the Confederate army, or, as *you* know him, Captain Walker, of the Federals!"

"Liar!" cried Hayward. "But no! I will not use such terms now. Do you know who struck the blow which so nearly deprived me of life?"

"Yes; it was William Nettleton! He is also enlisted in the service of Walker. And I will tell you more. In two days after you disappeared, Lieutenant Wells was hung for your murder. Your sister fled with Walker, who pretended the greatest friendship for her. *I* performed the ceremony, and to-night they are not three miles from you."

Hayward had become insensible, and sunk to the floor. Green saw this, and motioning to the old woman, they left him alone.

"That is the game I want *you* to play!" said Green, as they emerged from the mill. "Of course, all I have told him is false. But I want you to carry it out, because Colonel Price wishes it as well as Walker, and as he is a most dangerous man to our cause, I don't care how poorly he gets along. It would be a good thing for us if he could never take the field again. So see that you do your duty!"

Madge received her money, and agreed to follow all the instructions he had given her.

Green now returned at once to the camp, and reported to Walker. It was just before the decision of the court-martial had been given, and that officer was free, not only from restraint, but from any thing which had, as yet, assumed a definite form. He was delighted with the intelligence, and resolved to take advantage of it soon as Wells could be thoroughly crushed.

CHAPTER XI.

The Prison—The Wheel-room—Caged The Life and Death Struggle.

WE left Miss Hayward in the little boat, in the custody of Walker and stupid Dick. For several hours they sped rapidly onward with the stream. They encountered the party of rebels of which we have made mention, but, as Walker, or Colonel Brown, was the officer highest in rank, no one attempted to interfere with his project. The boat kept its course until it came upon a broad flat which appeared to be some five or six miles in length, and perhaps one in breadth. This, Walker informed Miss Hayward, was the "Valley of Bohannan!"

"And," said he, "your brother is confined in yonder mill!"

Miss Hayward gazed a moment upon the structure, and then burst forth in the same wild strain she had sung so frequently during her boat voyage.

"It is folly for you to attempt to attract his notice by your voice. He is a close prisoner and a maniac, and nothing but your constant presence and attention will ever cause his reason to return!"

"What do you intend to do with him and myself?" asked Miss Hayward.

"I intend to take you to your brother. I intend to let you see him in a wretched garret, with no hope of recovery, or of even life, unless you come to his aid. I intend to permit you to *gaze* upon this scene, but not even to speak with your brother, or to assist him in any manner, until you are my wife. Then you shall be free to attend to all his wants, to provide for his comfort, to restore him to reason, to life and to liberty."

Miss Hayward bent her head upon her hands and wept.

"I will not ask for your final decision now!" continued Walker. "I will wait until you have seen your brother, which will be in a few moments."

The boat was drawn to the shore, and Walker, turning to Dick, said:

"I will dispense with you now. Go to Joe's farm. Follow my instructions as to storing the house with provisions, and at least one comfortable bed. Miss Hayward, it is a beautiful place of which I speak, and, in case of your refusal to perform all that I wish voluntarily, or to save your brother, I shall be compelled to take advantage of a friend's mansion, in case I can not effect my escape with you to Arkansas. This I doubt being able to do, and more, I don't know that I shall run the risk, as I am only a subordinate, and some of my superiors *might* order your release. You perceive that I intend to make sure of my prize now that she is in my keeping. As my wife she will be permitted all proper liberty, but until you are such, by your own voluntary act, I must keep you safely from approach by any one."

Dick had left his master. Walker and Miss Hayward arrived at the log-hut adjoining the mill, and entered it. Old Madge was there, but she looked pale and frightened.

"Come here, Madge. What is the matter?" asked Walker.

"The devil's broke loose!" replied Madge, trembling violently.

"Come, don't be alarmed; I am Walker. I am the one who sent you the hundred dollars to keep the man safely. You have done so, I hope."

"He has just broke loose, and run into the woods."

"How did that happen?"

"Oh, he heard a voice singing outside, and, in his fever-delirium, said it was an angel calling him to heaven, and he burst from his room and rushed up yonder."

Walker and the old woman conversed together in undertones for a few moments, when he turned to Miss Hayward and said:

"Your brother, in his delirium, broke his chains, and is at large in the mountains. He will not return here, and I think it doubtful if I can find him. He will, most likely, make his way to the Federal camps. But, come with me; you shall see where he was confined, and then learn my further intentions."

Walker seized the unresisting maiden by the arm, and drew her into the mill. Up the dirty stairs she went, and finally entered the room, or attic, where the unfortunate brother had been detained prisoner. She shuddered as she gazed around her.

"Now," said Walker, "I will show you *your* room—one you shall occupy until you are Mrs. Colonel Brown."

He drew her still further on, and opened a massive door, which grated upon its hinges. She gazed in. It was a small apartment into which the carpenter usually entered when he wished to repair the great water-wheel which set the mill in motion. This room, or rather aperture, was of construction unlike any apartment intended for occupancy. There was a platform about ten feet in width, which formed the only flooring. Then a great opening beyond, through which the main wheel extended upward about eight or ten feet, entirely filling the opening in the floor. Any man confined in this apartment would find little difficulty in effecting his escape, provided he was an expert swimmer, and the mill not in motion. But the manner in which an escape must be effected would be as follows:

When the mill was running, the wheel being then in motion, the water was thrown in large quantities in every part of the room, and its inmate could scarcely prevent drowning by catching his breath at intervals. To attempt to spring into the wheel—which was formed something like the wheel of a wagon, the rim, or tire, however, being about twenty feet in breadth, with crevices, or brackets, for catching the water which propelled it, and the braces answering as spokes bearing proportion to the rim—would almost assuredly be dashed in pieces in the attempt to gain the interior. But, once there, he would be whirled round and round until he could gather his energies for a jump when that portion of the wheel in which he was perched was *down*, or nearest the bed of the stream. To leap out *into* the river would be a task equally perilous to that of springing in. When the wheel was *not* in motion, one could step into the opening, slide down the rim with great ease, spring into the water, and gain the shore in a moment.

Miss Hayward gazed into this room or vault with a fainting, sickening sensation; but she did not speak. It appeared as if hope had almost left her heart, now that she found her brother gone, and she nerved herself for any fate that might overtake her.

It was, as we have stated, late in the afternoon before the rebels encamped around the stack where Nettleton and Fall-leaf were secreted, took their departure, and up to that time the two faithful pursuers were unable to venture forth. At last all was safe, and they emerged from their concealment, and gazed around them. No living person was to be seen. A meal was hastily prepared, after partaking of which they resumed their journey at a rapid rate. All night they plodded along, taking care to see that no *mill* was passed upon the route. As the morning dawned, they found themselves in an open space of considerable extent, and close by the stream was a mill. This was carefully examined in every nook and corner; but nothing was found. They made inquiry of a woman living in a cabin near the spot, and learned that, a mile further on, was another mill of larger dimensions, belonging to one Bohannan. For this place they immediately bent their steps. Arriving, they were met by old Madge, who immediately commenced her mummeries in order to divert their attention. The Indian gazed upon her a moment, as if half in awe, and half in fear, but Nettleton did not pause, and exclaimed:

"Come along, Ingen; I expect here's the place."

They entered the mill. The Indian remained at the door to prevent any egress, while Nettleton commenced his search. Up and down, high and low, the search was prosecuted.

Walker being then within, had observed the approach of Nettleton and the Indian. His first impulse was to fire upon them; but he knew if his aim proved inaccurate he might then bid adieu to life, and so he resolved to resort to stratagem. He seized Miss Hayward and sprung into a wheat-bin, close by the door of the wheel-room we have described. He soon buried himself and his prisoner among a lot of old bags, husks and refuse, and cautioned her to remain quiet, as a band of Kansas cut-throats, who regarded neither the life or person of a pretty woman, were at hand. This had the effect to keep Miss Hayward quiet.

Nettleton had completed his search. The lower floor of the mill had been carefully scrutinized—its closets, its bins—except the small one near the wheel-room, which had escaped his notice.

"I wonder if there is any thing under the mill?" queried Nettleton. "I'll call, and see if that does any good. Captain! Captain Hayward!"

The voice was at once recognized by Miss Hayward, who vainly struggled to reply; but Walker held a handkerchief so tightly over her mouth that she could produce no sound. At length, by a desperate effort, she removed his hand and shrieked:

"Here, William! here!"

"Where? where?" cried William, as he sprung toward the bin.

"*In the wheel-room!*" yelled Walker, smothering his voice so far as to drown the exact direction in which it came.

Nettleton bounded into the wheel-room, closely followed by the Indian, who now supposed their friends to be found. Quick as lightning Walker sprung from the bin, and slammed the door upon them, bolting it securely. He then started for the mill-gate, which, being hoisted, would set the large wheel in motion.

As soon as the door was closed upon Nettleton, he rightly suspected treachery, and throwing himself with all his violence against the door, tried to force it. But in vain.

"Quick, Ingen; jump into the mill-wheel, and down into the water!"

They were about to adopt this plan of escape, when the wheel started with great rapidity, rendering it seemingly impossible to do so.

"Now," yelled Walker, as he seized Miss Mamie and bore her from the mill, "you shall see the folly of opposing me! You shall see how I triumph over *all* obstacles, and how those who oppose me perish!"

Inside of the mill, and near the door, was a quantity of hay and unthreshed grain, stored there for use by some neighboring farmer or guerrilla. Striking a match, Walker lit the inflammable material. In a moment it blazed high, and communicated with the woodwork. Walker only waited to see this, and then, almost dragging Miss Hayward along, he reached the river, drew the boat into the stream, and was once more floating with the current.

"Look, Miss Mamie, is not that a lovely sight?" he cried, pointing to the mill, now thoroughly enveloped in flames. "Nettleton is there, and Fall-leaf is there, and they have been brought there by *you*. They will perish in those flames, and you must be responsible for their murder. When will you learn that it is useless to oppose me, and cease to do so? To submit to my proper and honorable requests is the only way you can save your friends."

When Nettleton and Fall-leaf found their mode of escape thus cut off, they naturally turned to each other for advice. But the water thrown from the wheel so blinded and choked them that they could not hold conversation at all. It was not long before our prisoners became aware of the fact that, however disagreeable the water might be, they were likely to be visited by an element, and that very soon, far more disagreeable, under the present circumstances. The flames were seizing upon every part of the mill, and all around them soon became a mass of lurid, destroying light. The rafters, flooring and upper work threatened to fall at any moment. Still the room in which our friends were confined remained unscathed, surrounded as it was by water. But, it must soon yield to the fiery element. The wheel still moved; yet it seemed as if its speed was somewhat lessened. At length Nettleton yelled:

"Ingen, I'm going; take your chances!"

With a bound he sprung into the wheel. He escaped any severe blow, but, upon alighting he was tossed, and pitched, and tumbled over, until at last, catching upon the centre-bar, he held himself until he had made his calculation as to where his next jump should be. At last he ventured the hazardous leap, and was precipitated into the foaming waters beneath the wheel, which in its revolution struck him lightly, calling forth a grumble or a grunt. But Nettleton battled bravely with the rushing waters, and at length, half dead with suffocation, he crawled upon the bank as the burning rafters of the mill were falling around him.

"Wal, I suppose Ingen is roasted alive, and I must do the work alone. I'm darn sorry. And I've lost my gun, too. But I ought to be glad that I didn't lose myself. The villain, but won't I roast him if ever I lay these hands on him!"

Thus he muttered as he sat for a moment gazing upon the appalling spectacle before him. He then sprung up, and seeing the old woman, at once started for the cabin. Madge met him at the door.

"Will you have my services, to tell you truly the fortune that is in store for you?" she asked.

"Your services. Yaas; I'll have you tell me all about affairs here in this quarter, and if you don't own up every thing, I'll put you in this pile of logs and roast you, as sure as you are a she woman. Do you understand?"

"I have but little to reveal of the circumstances to which you refer. The Federal officer *was* in the mill a prisoner, but escaped, in his delirium, and is now somewhere out in the mountain. Walker and the lady were in the mill, but are now out of reach, down stream. This is all I know."

"And it is enough. Now, you just fork over a good Minié musket—I know you have a dozen concealed here for the use of your friends, and all the fixins for settlin' the hash of your friend, Captain Walker, for him and me has an account to fix what will require powder and lead, if this bread-cutter of mine don't do the job," he said, handling his bowie-knife.

Madge only too well read in Nettleton's face the resolute nature of the man, and with scarcely a moment's hesitancy went out of the hut to a hollow tree near by, and produced from thence an armful of arms, made up of shot-guns, old-fashioned rifles, and a Minié musket. From these Nettleton selected, after careful scrutiny, a heavy double-barrel squirrel gun. Ammunition was also supplied by the woman without hesitancy, and the pursuer soon found himself equipped in a most formidable manner.

"There, old gal, you have done the right thing. It is well that you did, for, as sure as lizards, I should have burned you in your pen if you hadn't forked over what I know'd was in your possession. Now, good-by, and behave yourself. If the captain—my captain I mean—comes back to you, do you be kind to him, for I tell *you* it is for your best interests to be so. Do you believe that?"

"I believe any thing you say," replied the old creature, betraying her anxiety to get rid of her visitor.

"You do, eh? Well, jist keep on thinking so, for I shall, mayhap, want to use you again some of these days. So good-by, and keep your eyes clean."

With this injunction he started again for the river, following the stream for some distance, but finally, for some reason best known to himself, took to the mountains. Every few moments he would pause and listen, as if a faint sound met his ears, and then continue his journey.

After Nettleton had escaped from the mill, Fall-leaf began to look around for some other means of escape. He felt sure that Nettleton's leap must be a fatal one—that, if he was not dashed to pieces by the wheel, he would surely be drowned in the rushing waters. All chance of escape for the poor Indian appeared quite as hopeless. The flames were already hissing around him, and curling up the sides of his prison-house. The fire had weakened the boards, and, just as the flames were coiling around his form, he made a desperate effort, and burst the siding from the mill. In an instant he sprung through the aperture, although the fiery element presented a formidable obstacle between himself and safety. He alighted, however, with only a few slight bruises, and, waiting for nothing, bounded forward. He knew if Walker had continued his journey down the river, he could soon overtake him. For an hour he did not slacken his pace, and finally, in turning a short bend in the river, he beheld the boat.

He was about to dash forward to the rescue of Miss Hayward, but he remembered that he had no gun, his only weapon being his sheath-knife, while Walker was well armed. He must resort to stratagem. His object was to watch for opportunity, and when Walker should land, or when the boat neared the shore, and the thicket favored the movement, to spring upon him suddenly, and drive the knife to his heart. But the river gradually grew wider, and Walker kept his boat in the center, too far distant from shore for any attempt for his seizure to prove successful. All that day and all the night following, the boat drifted on with the stream. It was evident Walker was anxious to reach a certain point as quickly as possible.

The morning dawned just as the little craft shot past the ford on the Rolla turnpike, near the "ghost swamp," a locality of weird interest and novel character. Walker was about to land, near a small farm-house which stood behind a jutting hill, entirely concealed from the main road, but before touching the shore, his quick eye caught sight of a dark form creeping cautiously along the bank. At the same moment he discovered three horses tied in a thicket only a short distance from the house. Whether they belonged to friend or foe he could not tell; but the fact of seeing the creeping form rendered him cautious, and he immediately pulled for the opposite shore, where he landed.

"Are you friend or foe to the Confederates?" shouted Walker, from the opposite side of the stream.

There was no response.

"That cursed Dick must have betrayed me," he muttered. "But, I will match them yet. Come!"

He dragged Miss Hayward along up the mountain steep. At length he reached a point of rock which extended far over the valley below. A narrow footway, not more than ten inches in width, forming a kind of shelf in the rock, led into an immense cavern, which is known in that region as the "Silver Cave." Just in front of this cave was a large, flat rock, forming an overhanging platform, but to reach this, or the mouth of the cave, required great care, as the narrow path was the only manner in which an entrance or exit could be effected. Into this place Walker conveyed Miss Hayward.

Walker had, when meeting the rebels two days before, provided his boat well with provisions. These he conveyed with him into the cavern.

He had not observed, however, that he was followed closely, and that the Indian arrived at the narrow passageway just as the rebel and his prisoner entered the cave. This was so. The Indian crept up as closely as possible, and peered over the projecting point which shut Walker from his view. He was observed.

"And who are you?" yelled Walker.

The Indian was perfectly familiar with the cave. He knew no person could leave it by the narrow shelf or pathway. He could keep himself concealed, and if Walker passed a certain point, before he could bring his gun to bear, he could strike him dead. Walker was a prisoner, with a watchful and relentless keeper. The Indian replied:

"Ah, White Bird! Fall-leaf here! Fall-leaf save!"

"Is it indeed my friend Fall-leaf?" cried Miss Hayward, joyfully.

"Yes; Fall-leaf save you!"

"Where is William Nettleton?" asked Mamie.

"Gone—gone!"

"Ah! then I have only *you* to encounter," yelled Walker, "and, if the Fates favor me, I shall triumph. I know the Indian has not thought to provide himself with provisions. I have enough to last us, with care, for two weeks, and by that time he will starve, for no Federal fool ever will find me *here*. He dare not leave in search of help, for I should then effect my escape. So we will play our hands, and see if I do not hold the trump card. Ha! ha! I can baffle any friend you have, Miss Hayward."

"White Bird sing," said the Indian.

"Yes, I will sing. And as we are now near the main road, some one will be sure to hear me."

"Me watch—me wait!"

During the entire passage Miss Hayward had not failed to sing her echo-song every few miles, hoping to attract attention and gain assistance. Now that she was so near the public highway, she applied herself anew to the task. Walker made frequent attempts to silence her, but could not do it, as he feared, whenever he turned from his watch, that the Indian would dart in upon him.

Some two years previous, there was a superstitious belief prevailing in that section of Missouri, that the spirit of a murdered lady appeared upon the waters of the Gasconade, singing her mournful lays, and gliding in her death-skiff along the waters. For some time past nothing had been heard of the "lady-ghost;" but, when the songs of Miss Hayward were heard, the simple inhabitants began to think that the "ghost-lady" had returned, and, instead of seeking to gratify their curiosity, were careful to keep as far as possible away. So it proved with regard to the cave, after the singing commenced.

Several days passed, and no succor appeared. The Indian kept faithful watch, and so did Walker, that he might not be taken by surprise.

Walker becoming convinced that Fall-leaf had no gun, several times endeavored to bring his own to bear upon his vigilant foe, but this he could not do without placing himself in a dangerous position. Both were weary for want of sleep, and both would occasionally sink into a fitful slumber; but, so intent was each upon his object, that the slightest movement would rouse the sleepers, and each stand ready to meet his foe. But, as Fall-leaf had no food, he began to grow faint—his firm frame began visibly to weaken; still, he determined to maintain his watch as long as life should last.

CHAPTER XII.

The Mountain Adventure.

LET us return to the army, which we left near Lebanon. The main force was to continue its march onward toward Rolla, while a battalion of infantry, a section of artillery, and a company of cavalry struck to the west of the main road, and started for the point from which the messenger had arrived. It was a weary march, as the troops already had proceeded twenty miles that day. But the dreadful atrocities related as having been committed by the guerrillas fired the hearts of the brave soldiers, and they pressed forward with a will.

The troops at last reached the scene of the outrages, in the place known as "Bohannan Mills Valley." The deeds of blood and horror had not been exaggerated by the messenger. Women had been murdered in their beds, old men were lying stiff and cold, with their brains beaten out, and children, helpless and weeping, were clinging to their dead bodies or wandering distractedly around.

The battalion which had been sent to this valley was the one to which Lieutenant Wells and Adjutant Hinton belonged. Wells was still suffering from the terrible anxiety of mind which he had recently undergone, but did not permit his own troubles to interfere with his discharge of duty. The troops camped in the little valley, to collect the scattered families, whose remaining members it was determined to take along with the army in its retreat. Soon word was brought by a mountaineer that the guerrillas still were infesting the mountain, while the flames of a burning mill, seen below, seemed to give evidence that the miscreants still were at their work of blood. This decided the officers to scour the mountain, if possible, to force the rebels to a fight, for there was not a man in the Union ranks who did not pant for a chance to meet those dastards, who, under the protecting folds of the Confederate flag, committed atrocities at which humanity stood aghast. Wells was soon at the head of a strong party of dismounted dragoons, and with them struck off for the hills back of the burning mill. A weary march was brought to a sudden halt by a deep water gully, over which no perceptible ford offered a passage. Up and down it Wells passed to reconnoiter. It was an ugly spot to be caught in by a wily foe, and the troops were so disposed as to guard against a surprise. The men kept close under cover of the dense undergrowth, so as not to betray their position should the guerrillas come upon them. Lieutenant Wells and Adjutant Hinton were proceeding up the watercourse, when a rattle of fire-arms arrested their attention. It was evident some kind of a conflict was taking place over the stream. The volley was not, however, answered by a return;

only a single shot was heard, and then a wild, frenzied shout, as if of maddened men. After a brief interval, another shot was heard, and a second paralyzed howl was followed by shouts and curses, plainly heard by the two anxious senior officers.

"It must be the guerrillas after the poor Unionists who have fled to the mountain," said Hinton. "Our men must not be idle when such work is going on. You stay here, Wells, to watch further, while I go back to bring up our boys."

Hinton hurried away, while Wells crept forward to the very edge of the deep but narrow gully beyond which the sounds of conflict were heard. Hardly had he secured a spot for observation, ere he was startled by the crash of the undergrowth and the voices of men not ten rods away. On toward the lieutenant's place of concealment came the pursued and pursuers. The first was but a single man, whom Wells several times detected gliding along from tree to tree, keeping "under cover" like an experienced woodsman. He was closely pursued by a band of the guerrillas, all dismounted, who were making the hills echo with their demoniac yells. Slowly the fugitive retired, holding his foes at bay by his sagacious maneuvers. Wells became intensely excited over the scene, and resolved to rush at once to the brave fellow's aid, but there lay before him the impassable gulf over which few men could bound. Finally the hunted man struck the gully, and saw at a glance that his retreat was cut off. The enemy saw it, too, for they set up a shout of commingled derision and pleasure, which so maddened the fugitive that he yelled:

"Laugh away, you darn skunks. I'll make more than one of your dirty carcasses food for the crows before I go under." And suiting the words to action, he fired two successive shots from what, apparently, was a double-barrel fowling-piece. Two of the guerrillas must have fallen, for ferocious shrieks of agony followed.

Wells could endure no more. There stood before him his brave friend William Nettleton, hunted by a dozen fiends who must soon overpower him if aid was not quickly given. He started backward for a couple of rods, then rushed with almost flying swiftness up to the gully, and bounded over its sharply-cut edge. For a moment his desperate leap arrested all attention. Nettleton deemed it a new adversary coming upon him from an unexpected quarter, and turned, knife in hand, to close in with his antagonist. What was his astonishment to welcome Lieutenant Wells to his arms! What a shout followed! The guerrillas quickly sought cover, not knowing how many others might be lurking on the opposite side of the ravine to give them a bloody welcome.

"Wells, by the jumping jingo! Where *did* you come from and where *is* you going to? Give us yer hand and lend us yer revolver. Ah, got two of 'em. *Hooray!* Down on yer knees quicker'n lightnin', for the woman-murderers are after us, sharp!"

Down the two men fell, just in time to escape a volley from the carbines of a squad of the murderers. With the dexterity of a squirrel, Nettleton rushed forward to a friendly tree, and fired quickly three shots from the revolver. It was a surprise to the enemy, for two of their number fell, so true had the aim been. The squad retreated to reload, but Nettleton had no idea of permitting that, and was about to press his advantage, when a powerfully-built rebel came rushing upon him, knife in hand, from the right side of the tree, unseen by the undaunted man until it was too late for the use of his fire-arm. In a moment they were clasped in the death-struggle. Three or four of the guerrillas rushed to the spot, only to be shot down by Wells' deliberate aim. No more appeared, and the two combatants were left to their fearful work. Each had seized the knife-hand of the other. Then followed the strain of muscle for the mastery. The guerrilla, counting upon his tremendous strength, doubtless hoped for an easy victory; but in that ungainly form he found a bundle of nerves tough as whale-bone—a human frame elastic as india-rubber but as invincible as steel.

Down toward the gully the combatants pressed. In vain did the rebel try to force his antagonist to the earth. The supple form of Nettleton bent under his adversary's pressure, but his frame at length rebounded with a force which bore the guerrilla to his knees. He drew the Federal down with him, and on their knees the frightful combat was continued. Wells would have advanced from his concealment to the rescue, but knew that a rebel carbine would surely bring him down, and thus place it out of his power to aid his friend at all. Slowly toward the chasm the men worked their way, struggling like two serpents striving for the death-triumph. It was an exciting but appalling spectacle, which the sudden roar of fire-arms on the left did not serve to arrest. A shout followed, which Wells recognized as that of his own men, who must have discovered a crossing below, and have come upon the band of cut-throats unawares. There was a sudden scattering of those concealed in the immediate vicinity of the hand-to-hand contest, but one villain rushed from his cover upon the writhing forms of the bleeding men, with the design of dispatching the unconquered Federal. Wells was upon him like a tiger, and in a moment cut him down with his sword. Hinton beheld the stroke, and came rushing up to the spot just in time to behold the struggling men go over the gully's bank together.

The two officers hurried to the bank. Some twenty feet below they could distinguish the forms of the combatants, both apparently lifeless. Without a moment's hesitancy, Wells dropped from the brink, and fell crashing through the dense jungle lining the water's edge, to the bed of the stream. He was stunned but not injured, and arose to his feet to find Nettleton in a sitting posture. Beside him lay the big guerrilla, silent in death.

"I'll be danged if that wan't the ugliest cuss as ever I tusseled with, breeches-holt, back-holt or rough-and-tumble." This was his first ejaculation.

"Are you injured?" anxiously inquired Wells.

"Wal, let's take a reconnoissance. Here's a hole in this arm, that's sp'iled the only good coat I ever had, dang it! Here's a rip, too, in the collar, whar that critter's knife tried to cut my windpipe. He *did* scratch me thar, I believe," he said, fingering his neck, down which the blood flowed freely. "By Jemima, ef I haven't lost a finger!" he added, suddenly holding up his hand. "Now, that's too bad, ef it is on the left hand. I rayther think the reb got a mouthful when he chawed that off!" And thus he would have continued for another ten minutes had not shouts from above aroused him.

"Who's come?" he asked.

"Hinton and the battalion."

"Glory! And have the rebs been caught in a trap?"

"I don't know how many, but from the shots and shouts I don't think many will be permitted to escape."

"All right. Now jist give us a lift, to see if my shanks is all right. There, that's the juniper. Jist look at my back, and see if you find any holes that want plugging."

No "holes" were found, and the good-natured fellow came out of the combat with only flesh-wounds, save the loss of one finger from the left hand, which the guerrilla had bitten off. Nettleton was much exhausted, and was finally drawn up out of the gully with no little difficulty, when the men set up a shout which made the hills ring.

"There, boys, that'll pay for the bruises; and now I guess you'll have to do me another favor—jist rub my shanks and the hinges in my back with a little whisky, if you can spare it."

In a moment a dozen pocket-flasks were produced and willing hands gave him a good rubbing, which gave his limbs new strength. It was evident that his muscles had been severely overtasked, for he was languid and incapable of exertion.

Nettleton now narrated the particulars of his and Fall-leaf's adventures. Soon the troops were out on the search for Captain Hayward, while, assisted by a couple of comrades, the wounded hero of the hour made his way down to the cabin of old Madge. The old creature received him kindly and at once bestirred herself to make him strong again. The air was soon odoriferous with the smell of distilling herbs.

A prolonged shout, ere long, came rolling down the hill. Nettleton was aroused from a sleep into which he had fallen. His two comrades at once hurried out to ascertain its cause. Old Madge paused in her toil and said:

"The captain's found, I s'pose."

"Hooray!" yelled the invalid, now an invalid no longer. Springing from his bed he rushed out, and away he went up the hills in the direction of the still continuing noise. His companions, astonished at his sudden recovery, followed, and all were soon lost to sight.

Harry Hayward was indeed found, and the cavalcade, bearing him on a rude litter, after a half-hour's time, made its appearance coming down the mountain. Nettleton was at his side, crying like a baby. Wells held the sick man's hand, while his face, still expressing anxiety, beamed with joy. Hayward was discovered hidden in a quiet, cool nook, where he lay in a very exhausted condition. He had, in his fever-delirium, broken away from Madge's custody, but, no sooner was he out in the cool shade of the trees and rocks than his mind became clear and composed. Weak and ill as he was he still had strength to seek a place of safety from pursuit, should it be attempted, as he supposed it would be. At nightfall he had determined to seek out some respectable looking farm-house, and on the morrow to cast himself upon the mercy of strangers, knowing that even though that stranger might be a foe he could not be more inhuman than men wearing the uniform of Confederate officers. But the sufferer was spared further efforts. The shouts and reports of fire-arms Hayward distinctly heard, and at once surmised that a Union force was at hand. When the men scattered in squads for the search through the mountain, the captain beheld one of the parties passing before his hiding-place. It was his moment of deliverance. He stepped out before the astonished soldiers, who, not recognizing the apparition, did not at once welcome him.

"My men, don't you know me?"

"Captain Hayward!" they shouted, as they rushed upon him, and clasped him in their arms.

He was borne toward Madge's cabin, to be welcomed on the way by the gathering men. Wells now appeared. The joy of that meeting can be surmised. The welkin was made to ring with the glad notes of the jubilant soldiers. These notes it was which aroused the sleeper in the cabin, and when at length he appeared, struggling wearily up the hill, the cavalcade paused to permit the overjoyed parties a few minutes of undisturbed greeting. Nettleton was not even talkative—a circumstance indicative of the depth of his feelings—and it was not until the captain was fully domiciled in the cabin, that he could consent to talk of the past and its painful incidents. He then narrated the events of Walker's plot, as we have here recorded them, ending with the tragedy of the mill. It was a revelation of intense but most painful interest to the sick man; but he bore the affliction of his sister's loss with great resolution, sustained by the conviction that He who doeth all things well would not permit the evil one to triumph.

CHAPTER XIII.

The Cave and the Contest for Life.

AFTER two days spent in the cabin, Nettleton became excessively uneasy. From something which had transpired, he conceived that old Madge knew more of Walker's whereabouts than she had yet confessed. This conviction, once formed, was but the prelude to action. Without informing any one of his purpose, he followed the old woman into the woods—whither she went in pursuit of her medicaments—having in his hands a stout rope. In a wild, retired spot, he confronted her.

"Look here, old critter, you're close-mouthed, when it would be better for your health to talk a little. Now, you jist tell me where Captain Walker has taken Miss Mamie. Talk straight, and not a gap in the fence."

"I don't know where he has gone," she answered, rather evasively.

"That is, you are a nat'ral-born know-nothing. Well, it will assist your memory, perhaps, to stretch your neck a little, jist to take the kinks out, you know; so pass your shock of tow into this 'ere noose, while I pull you up on that limb." And suiting the action to the word he flung the noose dextrously over her head. She was taken by surprise, and trembling in every limb, asked:

"Would you hang me?"

"Sartain as there's a tree and here's a rope."

"I don't know where Walker is, but I think he has a place of refuge down the river, near the Ghost Swamp. There is a cave in the river's bank, opposite to the swamp, where I know his confederates occasionally secrete themselves. He may have gone there; but, as he has been gone over two days, I don't see why he should be there now. It is my opinion, however, that Miss Mamie, as you call her, is there, as it is the best place to keep her."

"Ah, thank you, old Mrs. Crow's-foot. There is something more on your mind, isn't there?"

Madge looked at him inquiringly.

"I know all about your friend's visit; so do you jist play your cards right, or I'll catch ye niggin."

This allusion to her "friend" startled the old woman.

"He was no friend of mine; he came along on his own account, and I only gave him bread, as I give any one who is hungry."

"All right; only, what did he tell you?"

She hesitated. Nettleton gave the rope a twitch, and looked up at the limb. The hint was enough.

"The man said he was up from below on a scout. He was anxious to know what I knew about the voice of a woman which he said had been heard all along the river. He heard it distinctly as he passed the road along the river by the Ghost Swamp; others had heard it, and he believed that I could tell him as to its meaning. I told him it was a sign that he was singled out for death—that every person who heard it was called, and he might, therefore, make up his mind that his time was come. With that he left. I did not inform him of who was in my cabin, nor any thing about what had happened here. So I hope you will let me go, and frighten me no more."

Nettleton slowly lifted the noose from her neck, and, without another word, walked back to the cabin. He called out Lieutenant Wells, who was then watching at the captain's bedside, and the two friends held a long consultation together, which ended by an order for a guard of twenty to be ready for a night expedition.

By ten o'clock all were in readiness and on their way, taking the river path down stream. Wells was in command. Nettleton acted as scout and guide. All night long they pressed on, and daylight found them on the hills opposite the spot indicated by Madge as the locality of the cave in the bank. Asking Wells for his field-glass, Nettleton carefully scrutinized the river's bank opposite. After a short survey he suddenly exclaimed:

"*The Ingen*, as sure as Sacramento!"

"What do you say?" inquired Wells.

"Fall-leaf—see him—there he lays, and there is the cave. I'm blest if I know what to make of it. I supposed, *of course*, that that red-skin was roasted alive in the mill; but there he is, and here I goes."

So saying, down he dashed into the river, and forded its waters rapidly. Once on the opposite side, he hurried up the bank, and soon reached the ledge across which the Indian was lying. The poor fellow was but half conscious from over-fatigue and hunger, yet his eyes were fixed with cat-like vigilance upon the aperture of the cave, while his hand still firmly clasped the knife upon which he relied to do his deadly work.

Nettleton approached him silently, and touched his feet. At once the Indian looked behind him.

"Give Fall-leaf drink—quick!" was his hurried whisper, while the finger on his lip indicated silence.

Nettleton comprehended all at a glance. Passing his canteen and knapsack to Fall-leaf, he beheld the Indian drink and eat with satisfaction. Not a word passed between them.

"Good! Fall-leaf *much* weak; now strong again," he whispered.

"Where's Miss Mamie?"

The Indian pointed to the cavern.

"Walker, too?"

Fall-leaf nodded, and scowled so fiercely that Nettleton perceived the savage wanted no interference in his case.

"Shan't I do the job for ye?"

"No—Fall-leaf *mad*. Me kill 'em—you go way."

"That's the talk, Ingen. You shall have your man; but, Jerusalem, don't I ache to git my paws on him!"

A noise was now heard in the cave; it was Walker's voice. "I'll not permit you to sing, I again tell you. If those men crossing the river are Union soldiers, you shall not betray our whereabouts, and if Fall-leaf moves I'll shoot him!"

"Bah, you ornery cuss; *I'm* on your track now!" shouted Nettleton.

"William—dear William!" cried the captive woman, recognizing his voice.

"*Here!*" he responded, "and so chock full of the devil that if I don't get rid of it soon it will spile me. Walker, you dirty beast, dare you fight me?" he yelled.

"I dare fight any decent antagonist, but don't care to dirty my hands with you," was the reply.

"Oh, you nasty, miserable, thievin' woman-stealer, man-assassinator. I'll cook your breakfast for you, but Fall-leaf shall eat it; *he'll* dirty his hands with *you!*"

"I defy you and all your crew," growled the rebel. "If one of you dares to show your head, you are a dead man!"

"Blast yer picter, here's a head—shoot it!" cried Nettleton, sticking his head out in a manner to dare Walker's fire.

The scoundrel was prepared, and discharged his gun in an instant. Its report had not ceased its echo ere Fall-leaf, with a bound like a panther, dropped before the entrance of the hole. Walker stood there with knife in hand, to foil any such attempt to storm his castle. A quick blow with his foot sent the Indian headlong over the ledge.

"Try that on me," roared Nettleton, who, uninjured by the ball from Walker's musket, was at the Indian's heels.

No sooner said than done, and Nettleton received an unexpected blow in the bowels from the rebel's heavy boot which sent him almost instantly over the ledge after Fall-leaf.

That was the propitious moment for escape. Without a word to his captive, he passed out upon the ledge, and had nearly reached its terminus when Lieutenant Wells, followed by his men, confronted the desperate man. Drawing his revolver, Wells cried:

"Surrender or you are a dead man!"

"I never will surrender to you," was the fierce reply, as the now cornered desperado began slowly to retire, backward, to regain his stronghold.

He had retreated fully half-way to the entrance, when his heel caught in the rough floor of the ledge, and his balance was lost. For a moment he sought to regain his foothold, but, finding it gone, he gave a shout and leaped over the precipice.

The soldiers looked over the ledge and saw his form disappear in the trees beneath. Wells did not wait, but rushed to the cavern mouth.

"Miss Mamie."

A form darkened the passage, and within stood Miss Hayward, smiling and blushing as if just caught at her toilet.

With a cry of joy Wells entered and clasped her to his bosom.

"Safe and uninjured! Thank God—thank God!" answered the maiden.

"Safe and restored; and, thank God, your brother, too, is recovered, and is now in our hands, doing well!"

"Then I am happy, indeed!" she could only reply, while tears of joy checked further utterance.

Wells had entirely forgotten Walker, in his moment of sweet communion with his restored friend. But, a shout which came up from the depths below recalled him to duty. It was a wild Indian war-whoop; then a succession of ejaculations which the men could plainly distinguish.

"Go in, Ingen!" "Walk along, Walker, you darn skunk you!" "There, that's a good un, Ingen!" "Now another in the corn-crib!" "There he goes!" "Hooray for the Ingen!"

All well knew the meaning of this, and a number of the men hastened to the base of the cliff, by a long, roundabout path, which came up from the river at the ford below. They arrived to find Walker slain, and Fall-leaf badly cut in the face, arms and shoulders, but no serious wounds on the body. Nettleton stood over his friend, bathing his wounds in the clear waters of the river.

"Ingen's done for the cut-throat, sure. It was mean to shut me out; but it was his game, 'cause he treed it. I'd give all I'll ever be worth—"

"Would you give Sally?" put in one of the men.

"Dang Sally—no, dang my skin—that is, dang me if I wouldn't give my commission, boys, that's it! give my commission to have had the satisfaction of doin' Fall-leaf's work." Nettleton looked savagely at the body of the dead man, seeming to feel that he had made a personal sacrifice in permitting the Indian to kill his enemy.

It would appear that both Fall-leaf and Nettleton, when kicked off the ledge, fell at its foot without injury, as the base was banked up to a considerable distance with the decayed and water-soaked *débris* of the bank, down which they rolled into the water. They had recovered, and stepped out into the stream to look up to the ledge, when they beheld Wells and Walker confronted. In a moment the rebel staggered, and went bounding off the ledge, and, like his two antagonists, came tumbling and sliding down the declivity, landing at the water's brink upon his feet. There he was received by the Indian, with the wild whoop which startled those above. Nettleton, in honor bound not to interfere, stood by while the two fierce foes closed in deadly conflict. Walker, though a resolute and strong man, was not equal in a knife fight to the supple savage. After a few passes, Fall-leaf buried his knife in the rebel's bosom. Thus closed the career of a bad man—bad by nature, but rendered doubly bad by the cause which he espoused. To serve that cause he had to betray his country, desert his friends, stifle the voice of conscience, perjure his honor, become a hypocrite and a deceiver: after that, all other degrees of crime were easy.

Wells followed the men at length, and appeared on the spot. He was shocked at the sight before him, but conceded its justice. His own wish was to have secured Walker for trial and punishment according to military law; yet, it must be acknowledged that, many times, he felt like wreaking condign personal vengeance on the head of the man who had wrought so successfully in crime. He ordered the body to be buried in the *débris* at the foot of the cliff; and there it reposes to-day, with no monument save the cave above, which will long remain as a witness to the traitor's crime and traitor's doom.

CHAPTER XIV.

The Body-Guard's Sickness and Cure.

SLOWLY the party wended its way back to the mill. Just at nightfall it came in sight of the lowly hut which covered the treasure so dear to the heart of the rescued maiden. How her eager arms longed to clasp her brother's form to her bosom—how her ears longed for the sound of his voice! The wings of the swallow would have been slow for her pining soul; but the moment of reunion came at last—the dead was made alive, the lost restored. Miss Hayward, gallanted by Wells, pressed on ahead of the troop, and their panting steeds at length stood riderless before the cabin-door, for the riders had disappeared within.

The meeting of brother and sister was one of mingled pleasure and pain. Both had suffered so much that to think of it was pain. Captain Hayward was greatly emaciated. Loss of blood, fever, hunger and exposure would have ended a life less tenacious than his; but, despite his suffering, the presence of friends, the rescue of his sister, the anticipated happiness of her union with the man who had proven himself so well worthy of her—all conspired to give an elasticity to his spirits more potent than the infusions of herbs prepared by the not unskilled hands of old Madge, who, from an enemy, had, "by the force of couldn't help herself," as Nettleton declared, become a useful instrument at a critical moment.

And what about Nettleton? All day long after the morning's experience at the cave, he had plodded on soberly, somewhat absorbed in his own reflections. Behind him sat Fall-leaf, who, from his weak state, was well content to ride. The Indian, though perfectly silent and apparently indifferent to all things, now that his work was done, still was inwardly pleased at the rescue and the thought of the pleasure in store for the captain, of whose safety he had been informed by Nettleton; and he was quite willing to go into camp for a few days before putting out again on his endless scouts.

"Nettle be sick?" he at length asked of his companion.

"Not by a darn sight, Ingen?"

"Nettle *be* sick—Fall-leaf knows it!"

"You be danged to darnation, you red onion-head of a Delaware!" was the somewhat excited answer, as he turned in the saddle and stared the Indian in the face.

Fall-leaf smiled. "Nettle want physic—Miss Long give Nettle physic," he obstinately persisted.

"Now look here, Mr. Ingen, ef you wants to fight, jest you say so, and I'll be catawampussed ef I don't lick you wuss'n a nigger what's got a mad woman arter him!"

"Fall-leaf no want to fight Nettle. Maybe whip Nettle—den what Miss Long say?"

"Yoh—yoh! you mean, sneakin' son of a brick-kiln! Ef you don't stop that clapper in your head, I'll be switched ef I don't put a peg through it!" And he set his face firmly to the front, roweled the horse severely with his spurs, and dashed ahead at a speed quite uncomfortable to the provoking Delaware.

When the cavalcade reached the cabin, Nettleton did not obtrude himself upon the party within. For an hour or more they were alone. At length Hayward asked: "Where is my brave preserver? Why is he not here to enjoy our happiness? And Fall-leaf, too; I would thank him as he deserves, the noble and devoted savage."

Search was made. Fall-leaf was found out by the camp-fire, undergoing the process of the lotion-cure for his wounds, at the hands of Madge, who was carefully washing the bruised and cut flesh of the red-man. All inquiries for Nettleton were fruitless; he was not to be found. It was ascertained, at length, that his horse also was gone. Many were the surmises as to the cause of his absence, and fears were expressed for his safety.

Morning came, and the party, now rejoined by the entire battalion, prepared to move, by easy stages, from the valley toward the line of march pursued by the retreating army. Captain Hayward was made quite comfortable in a camp-wagon, with his sister for companion and nurse. Fall-leaf pushed out far ahead to scout and secure the command from surprise. Adjutant Hinton and Wells were tireless in their devotion to the comfort and safety of their charge. It was a pleasant journey—that week of slow progress toward Tipton. At length, however, the village hove in sight. The white tents dotting the hills and valleys proved that the division was there. While yet a long way off, a party of horsemen, accompanied by ladies, was seen dashing off at full speed toward the spot where the battalion had halted for its noon bivouac. Wells caught sight of the party, and with his glass made out the gaunt form of Nettleton far in advance. Behind him on the same horse rode a female, whose identity the officer could not fix. Nearer and nearer the horsemen came, until, after an exciting race, they dashed into the camp—Nettleton and Sally Long! They were received with a wild huzza from the entire troop, and none shouted louder than Nettleton himself.

"Hooray! hooray! By the eternal jingo!" he cried, leaping from the horse, and leaving Miss Sally sitting there alone, before the eyes of the joyous and excited troops. Making his way to the captain's "marquee"—as the men had named the wagon—he was welcomed by Hayward in a manner which quickly turned his servant's joy to mourning, for the embrace of real affection bestowed quite upset Nettleton's confidence.

"I'm nothin' but a great darn skunk, any how!" he exclaimed, as, breaking away from the captain's embrace, he started for his horse and the neglected Sally.

"Nettle be sick!"

He turned to behold Fall-leaf gazing upon him in mock compassion.

"Not by a danged sight, you infernal lump of glory!" he now shouted, as, clasping the Indian in his arms, he gave the red-man a hug which brought forth a grunt.

"Ugh! Nettle make Fall-leaf sick! Guess Nettle got full of Miss Sally now!"

"Yes, sar; and thar she is, in all her glory!" was the rejoinder, as the "body-guard" pointed, in evident pride, to the smiling woman.

"Gentlemen of the jury! let me present to you my wife—the dangdest sk— no, the most blissful woman you ever saw."

"Your *wife*!" exclaimed a dozen voices at once.

"Yes, my wife! Hitched to me tighter'n a handle to the jug, by Chaplain Disbrow, two days ago, by the eternal jingo!"

This was enough for the men. All order gave way before the hilarious uproar which followed. They pressed around Sally to offer their congratulations, which the delighted wife received with great good-nature and dignity, still sitting where she had been left—behind the saddle, on the horse.

At this moment the party first descried rode up. It was composed of Mrs. Hinton, Miss Morton and a number of friends eager to welcome the captain and his sister, of whose fortunes Nettleton had most unexpectedly, three days before, brought the news to camp. That it was a joyous meeting may well be assumed.

Does not our story here end? To say that Miss Mamie Hayward soon became Mrs. Wells, in the presence of the whole division—that a grand gala-day followed—is but half the truth, however; for, at the same time, another bridegroom was there in the form of the pale but happy Captain

Henry Hayward, who took to be his comforter and his much-needed nurse, the woman who loved him most truly—Miss Nettie Morton. It was, indeed, a most happy consummation of a drama which promised, at one time, to end only in sorrow and broken hearts.

Not the least happy of all that throng, nor the least noted, was

Nettleton, the Captain's Body-Guard.

Milton Keynes UK
Ingram Content Group UK Ltd.
UKHW030626061024
449204UK00004B/287